Unhindered

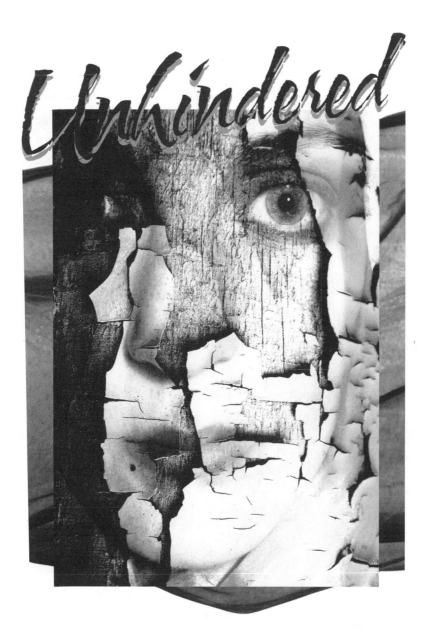

by Jana Spicka

Preaching the kingdom of God

and teaching concerning the Lord Jesus Christ

with all openness, unhindered.

Act 28:31

Unhindered, Revealing the Glory of a Woman
By Jana Spicka © 2007

Tree of Life Press
4815 Kingston Pike, Suite 145
Knoxville, Tennessee 37919

ISBN: 978-0-9727103-1-2

For more information on how to book conferences with Jana Spicka or to order additional **Unhindered** resources please visit:

www.janaspicka.com

Unhindered

Revealing the Glory of a Woman

Jana Spicka

Tree of Life Press

Knoxville, Tennessee

Dedication:

When my eight-year-old daughter asked if she could read my book I recalled the raw details and hard won victories recounted on these pages. "In due time you can. If no one else but you and Charis (my youngest daughter) reads this book that will be enough for me. You two are the reason I wrote it."

As I reflect further on my comment, it was completely sincere but not entirely true. This book is not just for my daughters, but for His daughters.

It is for all of us who are hurting and hopeless; for those who feel bewildered, abandoned, even trapped by our culture's definition of a woman.

His word says that weeping may endure for the night, but joy cometh in the morning. May this book lead you into the dawning of joy and freedom.

Acknowledgements:

Thank You Jesus for carrying me through every step of this journey. Just as You promised I am different and that makes all the difference.

And thank you:
To my husband Chuck for walking this journey with me. We often laugh and say we have been to hell and back a dozen times. But I love our life together. Through Him, we are still standing. Because of Him, you are the new generation of Spicka men, the ones who love their wives and stay with their families. I love you my Faithful friend.

To Debblie Patrick of VisionRun who had the guts to tell me that my "book" was a lot of good notes and thoughts — and to get busy. You are a great midwife. May God bless your incredible giftings a hundredfold.

To John Dee for his anointed teachings. Apart from the Lord himself, no person has impacted my relationship with God as much as you have.

To the interceding sisters: Nan Sprouse, Betsy Michalik, Christie Bethel, Melissa Fee, for praying and listening as I travailed over this project.

To the Michalik small group: the LeBoeufs, Rhodes, Morrells, Michaliks and Marshmans. You supported me much like Joshua and Aaron held up Moses' weary arms. You are dear to my soul.

To our college small group for being human guinea pigs and also for your passion for Christ. Never forget that you are a royal planting of our God.

To the team of intercessors and donors: you know who you are and what you have done, so does the Lord. May he richly reward your acts of love and faith.

To my now-scattered church family of CBC especially the Harrises, the Gilleys, and the Rileys, for shepherding us well. I love and miss you.

To my parents for believing that somehow God could and would redeem my broken life. You are the best grandparents in the world.

To my daughters Salem and Charis. Thanks for letting Mama pour time into this project. May you walk in the truth of your beauty.

Fathers be good
to your daughters
Daughters will love
like you do
Girls become lovers
who turn into mothers
So mothers be good
to your daughters too

1 — the question

"Mama, do I look pretty?"

There stood little Salem, my daughter. She was all dolled up as a flower girl in a magical wedding. She wore an ivory gown that laced up the back, just like the bride's, with petite brocade flowers and pearls along her hemline. Her blonde hair cascaded down her back and was clasped together with tiny, fresh rosebuds. Rose petals spilled out of the ivory vase she carried. And she was barefoot.

It was the perfect touch.

The ceremony was held on a warm, clear September evening in an outdoor garden. Natural beauty filled the eyes at every turn. The garden owners had spent the last eighteen years creating a wonderland — paths of blooming delights, gazebos and flower gardens, little pools and murmuring streams. It was an outdoor phenomenon.

The beauty of the garden plus the scent of rose petals and the sound of bagpipes hanging in the air made the whole evening almost surreal.

Or maybe, it was just *so real* that it took our breath away.

With only moments to spare before she was to precede the bride down the rose petal covered path, Salem ran over to me wide-eyed and intense.

"Mama, do I look pretty?"

She was five years old.

"No darlin'," I said choking back the tears. I squatted down and looked her straight in the eyes. "You don't LOOK pretty, you ARE pretty."

I knew this was a life or death moment in her little woman's heart. But I still winced from the thought—she's only five years old. *Where did this come from?*

Mirror, Mirror, on the Wall Who is the Fairest one of Them All?

I have had lots of piercing conversations, not only with my children, but also with the students I have taught for more than a decade. My teaching centers around the heartache of sex outside of marriage and the reward of sexual restraint. So needless to say, I have heard a lot of stories. I have heard the stories about why girls give their bodies away to boys — who in return give them mere moments of *feeling* desired and worthy of *love*. The drive for affirmation of beauty, of "looking pretty," drives young women straight into the arms of guys and then to despair. Girl after girl is crushed to find out that even though she has given her all — her virginity, her body, and her heart — it was not enough to keep the boy. Does this sound familiar?

These stories tear at my soul. Plus, I have two daughters who are, before my eyes, embarking on their own beauty quest. And finally, I have my own story. I have my own scars and medals from the beauty battle.

But through it all I have finally found something — or rather something has been *unveiled* to me about what I am, and who I am and who I am not.

The report from the journey to date is that I am finally good in my own skin and soul. I am beginning to taste freedom and see other women taste a freedom that is far more than we could ask or imagine. It's not easy, but it is oh so very worth the effort.

Will you walk a little of this journey with me? Let's see where the Lord leads.

In our first steps together, let me clarify what I am *not* talking about right up front.

I am *not* talking about "self-esteem" or "inner beauty" or any of the overused rationales that our culture harps on.

11

Let me explain.

Standing in a check-out line, I tried to explain to the high school-aged clerk why I was buying 1000 pink bags. "It's for a new event called 'The True Beauty Boot Camp,'" I said. She looked puzzled. "To help women realize their true beauty," I prodded.

She cocked her head slightly to the side and her eyes went blank. It was as if she had left the room to go fetch something. She snapped back to the present and rotely responded, "I think the more you have self-respect and the more you focus on your self-image and your inner beauty you don't get caught up in that sort of thing. You love yourself for who you are."

Impressive expression of thought. Where did she pull that line from? But more importantly, I had to wonder, who told her that she wasn't lovely?

"Yes, that's close" I said. "But I am talking about *God-image* rather than self image. You know as well as I do, that every woman looks every day in the mirror and wants to know if she is pretty. You cannot dismiss the longing. She wants to know the answer."

I leaned in a little toward her and smiled. "The answer is Yes. It really is *Yes*." She looked as if someone had slapped her.

So I am not talking about self-esteem or inner beauty or even outer beauty. Don't miss this.

I am talking about a *new source* to define beauty. She dismissed the definition of beauty and went off on a bunny trail of how to love yourself, regardless.

Regardless of what? Regardless of whether anyone else thinks you are pretty. My, my how subtle.

I am suggesting there is a new thought about Beauty in town. Out of this understanding we don't love ourselves in *spite* of our looks. We love ourselves BECAUSE of who we *are* in our true beauty.

What I am suggesting is an in-your-face, about your face, offensive posture. Think chicks with backbones for a change.

Our worth, and thus our worthiness of love, is not skin deep. It is in our very DNA. Guess what? Our worth lives right next to our beauty, which comes from a source that goes far deeper than the pages of *Cosmopolitan* and *Vogue*.

I am *not* talking about inner beauty.

Inner beauty has its place. It bears its own fruit. But there is more. Think about what happens after you hear somebody talk about "inner beauty." You get up and go straight to the ladies' bathroom and look in the mirror. You don't look for inner beauty. You look at your reflection. You are looking at you.

You want to know, *how do I look*?

Maybe you should ask instead, *how do I see*?

Not long ago, I sat in a women's meeting as two participants debated the appropriateness of frilly underwire bras versus all cotton sports bras. It was like the "natural woman" taking on a "runway wannabe." As I listened, one woman stated that there is freedom in Christianity for frills, (I quite agree) and the other spoke of freedom from the confines of what you must wear to be a woman (I quite agree). But I longed to scream, *what you are really saying is, can I be beautiful in my own way*? Unfortunately, I don't think they would have agreed with me. They were talking about concrete boxes. I am talking about colorful expressions.

There is a world of difference.

I am not talking about the do's and don't's of the Hollywood version of beauty.

There is a quest. There is more. But there is also a war.

We might feel it as we pass the magazine racks and inwardly groan.

We may feel it when we go to work, church, parties, and the mall. As soon as we walk in, we scan the room for other women, all the while mentally rating, grading and scaling them against ourselves. It is as if we have internal machines that compute for a moment, then go "ting" in our heads.

A receipt prints out in our hearts that says, "here is how you rate today."

There is more to us than external ratings.

This is why I want to tell you my story, as well as the stories of other women who are on this journey with me. I want to talk about the men who breathe life and the men who steal it from the deepest regions of our hearts.

Let's go to another garden of near magical beauty.

Once upon a time there was a Warrior and a Beauty. They lived in a garden. The garden was rich with the fragrance of flowers and ripe fruit and the sounds of birds and animals playing nearby. The couple feasted their eyes on the magnificent colors of beast and blossom and tree. They delighted in all this and in each other.

Of all the breathless creations, the Warrior and the Beauty were the crowning glory. Together, they were the masterpiece. Every creature and living thing the Good Creator spoke into place. But for the Warrior, he put his own fingers in the dust and shaped the man. Then the Creator reached down, mouth to mouth, and breathed life into him. The Beauty, last of all creations, the Creator fashioned with precision and perfection. The Warrior and Beauty he shaped with His own hands. And the created walked with their Creator in the cool of the eve.

Yet as they laughed and talked there were other eyes watching from the shadows. The eyes narrowed in a boiling rage.

For in the garden there was also a villain. The villain waited and plotted and schemed for a way to break the strength of the Warrior and steal the glory from the Beauty. Most of all the villain sought to wound the Creator.

In due time, opportunity availed. The villain came to the Beauty and began asking questions...

The same villain has been asking the same questions ever since.

Did God really say that?

Satan came to challenge the truth. (Genesis 3:1) He brought doubt. He had nothing else. But by questioning God, by offering something off limits, something he had no authority to give, Satan stirred the woman and the man to doubt the goodness of God.

In that moment, for of all mankind, the woman and the man who was with her, had to decide whom they trusted. Did they trust in their own beauty, their own strength, or did they trust the One who created them?

Satan tempted them to trust themselves, to take what they wanted for themselves. Instead of asking God directly, which they could have done, they tried to second-guess God's heart, His plan, His ways. They thought God was somehow withholding good from them. Ultimately they doubted God's love for them and lost more than they could imagine.

What is the big deal about a bite you might ask? Remember there were two trees, the tree of life, and the tree of the knowledge of good and evil. Satan did not offer a fruit from the tree of life. Why not? Because this would have been the first and last taste of total abandon and dependency on God. He *is* life.

Instead, Satan offered the fruit of *knowledge* of good and evil, of *self*-awareness. They would not surely die, he bantered. They took the bait and made an attempt to try to figure out life on their own, apart from God. They trusted God's *gifts* to be enough to see them through, instead of their *relationship* to the Gift-giver. They chose the seduction of strength and beauty over intimacy with their maker.

Looking back into their sublime little pocket of time, it seems insane to me that they would have doubted the heart of their Father. But what about us today? Who or what do we trust?

We are far from the garden, and even on this side of

the cross. We have the Holy Spirit to lead and guide. Yet we still bank on our own strength and beauty to be our indicators of life, of who we are.

When you doubt the love of your Creator, you lose far more than you know — just as Adam and Eve did. You don't lose His love. You lose your foundation of truth, the definition of you.

You doubt your own value because you have lost your source. So you must take issues into your own hands. Naturally, you grab at the fruit, because your definition and value system are up to you. Then, instead of running back to the arms that made you, you take a bite.

When you take a bite, you then have to take into your own hands the weighty responsibility of answering the toughest questions: Who am I? Why am I here? Does anyone care? We try to make ourselves be the god who can silence the doubt.

We are fools.

2 — white as snow

One of the most beautiful visual pictures of the garden of Eden is found in the least likely of places, Disney's production of *Snow White*. Go back and watch it again.

Take in the first wonderful scenes of Neuschwanstein's castle, and watch the wicked queen assessing her beauty in the Magic Mirror.

You know how is goes. 'Mirror mirror on the wall, who is the fairest one of all?' When the answer comes back 'not you, but Snow White,' she is enraged. She comes out with a classic hiss of "Blast her!"

Stop there.

I believe a lot of us live right here.

We never want to think of ourselves as the evil queen, but we do keep asking "mirror, mirror" and when the answer comes back favoring someone else — we are enraged or depressed. We tuck more, eat less, work out more, cover less. We will do almost anything to help tip the scales in our favor.

Or worse, when we realize we are not the fairest, we simply give up. We binge more, cringe more, shrug it off like it doesn't matter anyway. Are any of these responses so very different from "Blast her!"?

But who else does the queen sound like? Who in a very real tale, wanted to be the fairest one of all? Satan wanted to be the MOST beautiful. He recognized the value of beauty. He recognized *his* beauty. But his downfall was that he wanted to be the *source* of beauty. Satan wanted to be like God. His quest led him to the curse. It is the same curse he led us into. His quest didn't work for him and it won't work for us.

The sad but ironic truth is that we settle for lives that look like Satan's, chasing after what we can't have, when we have been given so much more, something so real.

If you are like I was at the beginning of this journey, as you read that last sentence you might be asking what exactly would *more* be?

"So God created man in his own image, in the image of God he created him; male and female he created them." (Genesis 1:27)

Did God really say that and the thousand other promises of who He is and thus who we are?

His image. God created man in His image. He created woman in His image. We are pictures, reflections, expressions of God.

Before you yawn, go back one or two sentences. We don't have to **try** to be someone. We already **are** someone. The problem is, we are blind to who that *someone* really is.

Of course we have had a little help being blinded.

The False God

The hundred-plus females entered the room, all twittering, as only girls can. There were young and old, leaders and students and the air was thick with curiosity. "What are we doing here anyway?" was the question.

It was the first True Beauty Boot Camp.

We showed pictures on huge screens and let the images fill their minds of long lean legs, firm curved bellies, too thin arms, polished glowing skin, pouty lips. One ad called it, "Kissable Lips." On and on flashed the definition of beauty according to Hollywood.

In deadly silence, we paid homage to The Hollywood god.

When it was over, you could almost hear the collective sigh. We tried to laugh it off. We tried to ignore the unnamed discomfort. We told ourselves it doesn't matter. We told ourselves we didn't care.

We lie about other things, too.

There it was. You could feel it. We all did. Regardless of age, shape or size, there was something from deep inside us, a haunting, calling out. It grabbed at those images and rubbed our faces in the comparison. It first scoffed in a whisper but then screamed in scorn, laughing at the far distance between Hollywood's supposed perfection and our reality. But then in a pathetic twist, "it" wanted, demanded, begged for, longed for someone to put us, put *our* pictures, on the screen and say— you've got what it takes, you've got the look.

Where did that haunting come from? The younger girls, in middle school and high school, were full of hope that they were well on their way to obtaining, somehow, the look. But those college-aged and older had already tasted enough rejection, the hook was already set so deep, that the haunting just pushed the jagged edge in a little deeper.

The silence hung for a moment. Reveal *truth*, I said in a whisper prayer. And then I asked the young women, "Do you feel that? Are you sick of it yet? Are you tired of being squeezed?"

My challenge to them, and to you, is will you take a cold hard look at where the haunting comes from? Who calls the shots? Whose *look* are we after? Who are we asking? Who is our Magic Mirror?

It is not the Beauty Maker.

It is the Beauty Idol. The false and consuming god.

The Hollywood god is very, very fickle. I am not complaining about the fashion trends. (Yet.) But we displayed magazine clips of the best- and worst-dressed, the fashion victors and victims, and oh, how ruthless the media is.

As the more recent fashions intersected with attendees

of the camp, you could hear the frustrated groan, "Did I really wear that?" Yes, you did. And you will. Because someone said it would make you beautiful if you did, or worse, make you ugly if you didn't.

One personal favorite of mine was the magazine article trashing the hip bone flashing jeans and how, now, that was oh so "yuck." Poor Britney Spears took a pretty bad beating. The irony is, it was this same magazine that had demanded just the year before that she (and we) wear this style or be out of the game!

My point is that this blind obedience is only testimony to the verse, "all we like sheep are led astray"— only we call it high fashion. (Isaiah 53:6)

We are constantly evaluating — either by pats on the back or stabs in the back — how we all measure up according to the fad of the day. Donald Miller in *Blue Like Jazz* went so far as to call our looks-driven obsession, the "worship of the god of Cool."

One magazine claimed to define "The Perfect Body." You see this composite about every other month only with a different assortment of celebrity names and body parts attached. This particular issue said the perfect body consisted of: amazing abs like Jennifer Lopez, sexy butt and legs like Heidi Klum, and awesome arms like Jennifer Garner.

Deep in my soul I knew I was making progress, because instead of trying to figure out how on earth I was going to duplicate their collage of body parts, I laughed.

"Goodness," I said out loud. "Last time I looked, I had Jana Spicka abs, Jana Spicka arms, and a Jana Spicka butt. I'm good."

Do you get it?

We have gone from being 'the best you can possibly be' to trying be all we were never *supposed* to be.

Where did we go wrong?

Let's go back to the garden where the Beauty and Warrior lived in peace. Remember the eyes? They incited a revolt. The result was — and continues to be — war. Think terrorism, guerilla warfare. Think weapons of mass destruction. The enemy's poisonous propaganda is being spewed over the airwaves.

> *Tell a lie loud enough and long enough and*
> *people will believe it.*

Do you see the alarm of that statement? Do you know who said that?

Adolf Hitler.

What we believe or whom we believe can have life or death consequences.

In my day-to-day life, what I hear on the airwaves, in magazines, through television and movies, is that I don't measure up. I won't measure up. I can't measure up.

This is not from a lack of trying.

3 — reruns

My middle school and high school years were spent being on the outside of the pretty girls. You know who I am talking about. The ones who have the clothes, the bodies, *the look*. In high school, I was pretty sure that you had to be a certain size, a certain height, with a pretty good cup size and blond hair to make the cut. Unfortunately, I was a brunette with no cup size. Needless to say, I did not make the cut. But I wanted someone to prove me wrong.

Either out of wishful thinking or desperate need, I entered beauty contests to try to prove to myself that I did indeed have *the look*. You have probably already guessed: four years of contests, no first place ribbons. Actually, make that no ribbons. My only moment of glory was when the dress my mom and I made won "best dress." But even then it was the dress and not *me* that got the ribbon.

Please understand that I was ambitious, bright, and had lots of talent, but that unknown haunting remained. I was looking for someone, anyone, to define me, to declare my beauty. So how do you go from freshman through senior year without winning a ribbon and still hold on to your heart? To my dismay, the winners were all brunettes. It wasn't my hair color after all. I concluded that there had to be something wrong with *me*.

College was a different story.

A funny thing happened on the way to class one day. I was walking with a girlfriend and nearby, underneath a huge tree was a gathering of campus males. From a distance you could hear a variety of whoops and hollers, barks and howls. Another girl, with her red face nearly buried in her books, walked as fast as she could past the crowd of boys.

"How gross," I said to my new friend, "why are they making fun of that girl?"

With an almost wistful tone, she told me they were not making fun of her, they are saying they liked what they saw. "Just watch," she said.

I did watch as several other girls walked randomly past the rowdy pack of testosterone. There was an eerie silence.

"See," she explained, "they only bark if you look good."

"It's still gross," I said lamely.

Two days later, I was walking to English class, lost in my own thoughts. The barking and howling quickly brought me back to reality. I looked around to see who the lucky victim was today. When I turned to face the mass of males, I was greeted with even more howling.

No way. My mind raced. No. Way. I realized I was the only girl in sight.

That's the day my addiction began. I was instantly addicted to the rush of getting someone to notice me. Oh, I turned red for sure, but I also flashed them a beauty pageant smile. The howls increased. And so did my love affair with male attention.

Like all addictions, it started out really small, nearly insignificant. "Harmless" really. But as time passed, it would take more and more of the addictive substance to get a rush or high or buzz. Plus, I was willing to pay a higher and higher a cost to get it.

That short-lived season on campus marked me in ways I didn't even know at the time. Because finally, somehow, I had gotten *the look*.

Of course I had no idea what *the look* was since I still had brown hair and no cup size. And I also had no idea that it was as fleeting as football season itself.

However. I was instantly aware of the *weight* of *the look*.

The hard reality is that if you have *the look*, you have to carry it around. All the time you have to keep it up. Keep it going. Be on display. At all times. You have to be "ready to be seen," if you will. The public and the addiction demand it. So whatever self-consciousness I was already dragging around, the pressure of looking good just added a couple more tons.

When I think of that season of my life, I hear David Bowie's song ringing in my head,

"Ch-ch-ch-changes..."

After all, college days come and go and so does your body. The problem is the addiction stayed.

Today I can tell you that I have been in bombshell shape and in pathetic shape. I have worn single-digit clothes and clothes with lots of Xs. I have eaten well and gone as far as eating disorder mania. I have had four pregnancies, two children, and one divorce, and presently have one husband that loves me but has not always been delighted in my appearance. That is the trauma.

But in addition to trauma is the *drama*. I lived in a swirl of excuses — rejection, perfectionism, control issues, fear. Lots and lots of drama. Both the trauma and drama were consequences of bowing before the Hollywood god. But it wasn't until I changed *who* I was asking, and *what* I was asking that the addiction was broken. The poison of the haunting was revealed. And once revealed, the poison was able to be sucked out.

There is a war for our beauty. There is a haunting. But the good news is "there is a deeper magic still."

In the *Chronicles of Narnia* series by C.S. Lewis, there is a character called the White Witch. She is beautiful and evil.

She knows her time is doomed when four children arrive in Narnia, the land over which she has seized control. In a game of wits, she tricks one of the children, and thus has a right to his blood.

The White Witch approaches Aslan the Lion, the true king of Narnia, with her demand for the boy's life and blood in accordance to the law of the stone table. However, Aslan forfeits his life to save the boy, to the delight of the

White Witch. Aslan had long been her enemy and threat.

As she stands over his bound and shaved body, ready to plunge the knife, she is all but overcome at the implication of the moment. Her greatest enemy is ready to die on the stone table. The knife drives into the great lion's heart. His eyes close in death. They leave his lifeless mass on the stone table. She goes off to finish the war on Aslan's kingdom.

But as the morning rises, there is a great crack in the stone table and it breaks in two. Aslan returns to life and is even more beautiful and powerful than before. Through his sacrificial death, Aslan has defeated the White Witch once and for all.

He explains to the children, that "although the White Witch knew Deep Magic, there is a deeper magic still..."

There is a deeper magic still for us too. This deeper magic brings freedom and life.

4 — face beauty

Don't let the world around you squeeze you into its own mold, but let God re-make you so that your whole attitude of mind is changed." Romans 12:2 (Phillips)

Why do you think the Lord has Romans 12:2 in the Bible? Don't be squeezed anymore into the world's mold. Think paper dolls. Think cookie cutters. Are you saying not guilty? Think hot pants. Bell bottoms. Farrah Fawcett hair cuts. Thongs. Belly button piercings. Barbed wire tattoos. Think brown hair colored with 700 shades of blond streaks. Don't even get me started on the name brands. All this and more so we will squeeze into the mold.

Think of the fear of showing up and looking "different." Are you sick of being squeezed yet?

Read it again from the NIV.

Do not conform any longer to the pattern of this world, but be transformed by the renewing of your mind. (Romans 12:2)

The invitation is to be transformed. Becoming something altogether *better.* Think cocoon to butterfly. Think caged to free. Think ball and chain vs. barefoot dancing. Think released.

You see, we can't help but be different, because we ARE

different.

Why? Because God is so creative, so powerful, so beautiful, so awesome, that even with 7 billion people on the earth, there is a unique expression of Him in each of us. In His image, remember?

Part of my own journey has been to ask the same question as the evil queen, "Who is the fairest one of all?" The only difference is that I stopped asking myself for the answer. I stopped asking the magic mirror. I stopped asking the Hollywood god. Instead, I went back to the Beauty Expert.

In fact, He is the Beauty Maker.

I am going to share the specifics of the journey but I want to give you the antidote to the snake bite now. You see we have all been bitten by a cruel and evil snake. You'll see that clearly and directly in my story, and perhaps in your own. But there is an antidote. Do you know what an antidote is?

> *Antidote: a remedy that stops or controls the effects of a poison.*

We have been poisoned alright. And we need something more than pat answers to stop the slow painful death it can cause.

The Antidote

The king is enthralled by your beauty. Psalm 45:11

When I first came in contact with this verse, I read it and went off thinking about King David and his billion wives. Oh, he loved his wives. That's just great.

Later when the verse came around again, a different teacher asked me to read it out loud. I did and thought to myself, "Isn't that nice. How special. Next."

I was looking at the wrong king. Because it is really serious business. The next time the verse came around, it was spoken *to* me. Directly. By the capital "K" king.

I didn't know what "enthralled" meant. So I grabbed a dictionary.

Shall I tell you? "To hold spellbound." To be so captured as to stop dead in your tracks. Hmmmm. Does that mean He sees me and can't take His eyes off me?

Wait — who's He? Are we talking about "Gawd" here? The Charlton Heston burning-bush God being stopped in His tracks over me?

Nah...that's not for me. I'm a loser. Everything around me tells me, 'Yep, you're a loser.' Once I could earn that kind of look, maybe, but not anymore. How about you? Do you think this verse suits you?

It sounds almost sacrilegious at worst, or at the very least, too good to be true. But there it is. In black and white.

God kept bringing that verse back to me. He just would not let me blow past it. I would stumble and fumble over it. I would say this just doesn't apply it to me. But one day I asked the Lord for Scripture to confirm Scripture, figuring that would silence the buzz in my heart. The Lord gave me *Behold you are fair my love.* (Song of Songs 4:1, KJV) And if that is not hard enough to swallow He told me over and over that *He delights in me* (Song of Songs 7:6, Proverbs 8:31, NASB)

Care to take a stab at what 'delights' means?

"Something that gives great pleasure or enjoyment..."

Me? He gets pleasure and enjoyment from me? Are you kidding? Oh you mean like all the things I *do* for the church, the kingdom? Okay, okay, I'm good with that. I show Jesus I love Him by serving, serving, serving and He is pleased with that.

Wait a minute. That is not what He said.

"The king is enthralled by your beauty."

He is enthralled not with what I do but with *me*. With my beauty. Your beauty.

Stop. Let that sink in. The king is enthralled by your beauty. Look at some other translations of this verse.

So shall the king greatly desire thy beauty... KJV
Your royal husband delights in your beauty...NLT.
The King is wild for your beauty... MSG

28

Maybe you missed that Royal Husband business just like I did. But what it says is, if I belong to Christ, which I do, then He is *"wild"* for this beauty.

My beauty. Your beauty.

Think howling and barking.

Right now. Not if we lose a few pounds or get that haircut. Not when we get *the look*. He feels that way right now. How can that be true?

The more I began to go to Jesus about what this means, the more disturbed I got. I shook my head in disbelief. I shook my fist because I had been hurt so much. But the more I shook, the more the shackles clattered to the ground.

I felt very alone at the time, but now I don't think I am the only one with these feelings. What about you? Have you ever thought that God was talking to everybody, anybody, but you? Me too. I hope you love His surprise answer as much as I did.

5 — back to the basics

In the True Beauty Boot Camps, I have each young woman do a craft. They come out of the room with a little creation of their own. Each person begins with the same ingredients but the end results are very diverse. No two are ever exactly alike.

I ask them to hold up their creations. I ask them to study their creations and tell me what they notice.

No matter how many times I do this, regardless of race, age or economic status, the observations are the same. Each creation is very different. Each creation is very pretty. Each young woman likes her own creation the best.

When I press them as to why they like it so much, the answer is always, *always* the same. "Because I made it. It's an expression of me."

In the image of God He created him; male and female He created them. (Genesis 1:27)

"Everyone who is called by my name, whom I created for my glory, whom I formed and made." (Isaiah 43:7)

Psalm 139 says that we are fearfully and wonderfully made.

Maybe that is why He likes you, and likes me, so very much. It doesn't say that if you've got the look you are fearfully and wonderfully made. It says that God don't make no junk.

So you see then, when we walk in a room and elevate or disqualify someone based on their looks, when we elevate or disqualify *ourselves* based on looks, we have thrown our fist in the air and said, God you screwed up. This face, this image, this *expression of you* doesn't make the cut.

Wonder what the Lord thinks about us trashing His "little creations" that He enjoys so very much?

He is the king. He is enthralled. He really delights in your beauty. Really. Why? *Because He made you and only you to express a facet of Him like no one else can.*

Are you thinking 7 billion people and each one an expression of God? I hope so. Because if you are, you might be just barely beginning to see how big God is. He knows us. He made us.

For all of our scientific prowess, Psalm 147 says He placed the stars in the heavens and knows them by name. The stars are not made in His image, yet they have a name. They reflect His glory for sure. But not in the same way His glory twinkles in our eyes.

God's kids look like their Dad. And God doesn't look like junk.

Are you struggling here? Ever notice that we will believe the Bible when it talks about salvation, the cross, the resurrection, even promises of provision. But when it comes to those uncomfortable places— like beauty, pleasure, relationship, intimacy — it's like somebody changed the station right in the middle of your favorite song.

God is far more than a supermarket. We don't go to Him to pick up a few things we need. He is the CREATOR. Author. Finisher. King. Bridegroom. So when He says "you're beautiful," what do we do with that?

'If' He is who He says He is, 'if' He means what He says, and 'if' He thinks I am a beauty, then my whole world has to shift.

Why is it so hard to do?   Why is it so hard to believe?

Snake Bites

Remember the eyes conjuring up evil as he watched the Beauty and the Warrior? They are the eyes of a serpent, and they are ever on the prowl. He cannot take away the truth of our identity, but he can cover it with lies, lies, lies. And if we hear a lie loud enough and long enough, we will believe it.

I have changed all the names, but these are very real wounds, very deep snake bites.

My friend Pam told me that her Dad said that he would pay her $10 if she would lose 10 pounds. She was in great shape, an athlete, but not the willowy idea he had for a daughter.

Jenny was tormented by an abusive boyfriend. He told her how unworthy she was since she had given her virginity to someone else before him. Add to this insult, his blind eye to his porn addiction. As if these didn't cut deep enough, he added, "I think you will look terrible in a wedding gown."

My friend Mary was babysitting a five year old little girl. Mary suggested that they put on some worship music and dance. The little girl immediately rolled up her shirt so that her belly showed and twisted it to make it tight and began a variety of bump and grind moves. Diva dancing was her idea of worship.

Lisa's mother was socialite, and her sister was a perfect size 2. When it was time to carry on the tradition of rushing for sororities, Lisa's mother told her, "You are too fat to rush. No one will pick you." Lisa's bulimia started immediately afterward.

Elizabeth had suffered through years of her husband's pornography addiction. She was in good health and great shape from walking, but her self-esteem was at an all time low. About that time, her husband said he wished she would work out more. "You would look a lot better if you would firm up," he said.

Callie was told by one of her passing lovers, "If you just had bigger boobs you would have a good body."

Caroline had made a heroic effort to lose weight. In fact she worked out six days a week and had lost over 100 pounds. When she went to a family gathering, her thin mother criticized her and told her to put on long pants.

"You should never wear shorts, you just don't have the body for it," she said.

You've probably got a few stories like these too.

Of all my personal snake bites, one that really hangs in my head is the comment from one of my very cool high school-aged brothers. When you are in middle school and you have cool brothers, what they say matters. A lot. So it cut to the core to be told repeatedly, "You have a such a fat ass." Add to that bite my late-blooming breasts in a family of "well-endowed" women. If cleavage meant that you were well-equipped and gifted (in my family it did), and I have no cleavage, what did that say about me?

We hear assessments, preferences, and evaluations every day.

We live in a world that makes a woman a cafeteria instead of an image of God. A little more here, a little less there, thank you.

Steeping in lies like this does something to your brain. Just look at how we typically deal with them. We cope in two ways. We either think (1) we can beat the system — and we work and work and work to do so, or (2) the system beats us to a pulp.

A third way may be to bounce between 1 and 2 frantically.

All of us have some kind of lie lodged in our brain. Fang marks.

We either push and push to overcome the lie or we shut down. We see the stars on the magazine covers and wonder can I really lose 10 pounds in 10 days? Bulimia. Anorexia. Work-out compulsion. Or overeating and obesity. All of these are reactions to the poison spreading through our systems from the snake bites.

We have been gassed so much by the chemical warfare that we are paralyzed. Our brains have been programmed to believe that *you are worth loving if you look right.* If you don't, forget it.

But remember the antidote? The King is enthralled by your beauty.

1) If He is who He says He is.

2) If He means what He says.

3) If He thinks I am a beauty.

These are three pretty significant *if* statements. At some point, you will have to decide where you square with the Bible. For me, I believe it all. It is the most historically documented book of all time. There is more evidence confirming its contents than records of great historical figures. Lee Strobel's book *The Case for Christ* says there is more evidence that Christ is who the Bible says He is than there is evidence for Alexander the Great. No one doubts who Alexander was and what he did. But more than the scholarly head knowledge, I have experienced the Spirit of God moving in and through the Scriptures to teach, comfort, redeem, change and help me. He will do this for you too. That's just how He is.

So let's walk this out.

If He is who He says He is: I really believe we don't know who we are because we don't know who God is. When Satan tempted the woman and man to take a bite, it was a bite of knowledge of self-discovery, self-awareness. Self.

We try to define ourselves by what we know. We go through mental exercises, we read and explore and talk and vomit and distort and learn and forget. You get the picture. We are quite busy with intellectual endeavors. I call it studying our navels. Navels are neither very deep, nor very compelling. All I have ever found in my own is lint.

But, "Oh the depths of the riches of the wisdom and the knowledge of God. How unsearchable his judgments and his paths beyond tracing out." (Romans 11:33)

The knowledge of God is powerful, mind-blowing, life-changing.

Paul cried out a prayer for the Ephesians, and for us, that out of the Father's glorious riches "he may strengthen you with power through his Spirit in your inner being, so that

Christ may dwell in your hearts through faith. And I pray that you, being rooted and established in love, may have power, together with all the saints, to grasp how wide and long and high and deep is the love of Christ, and *to know this love that surpasses knowledge* – that you may be filled to the measure of all the fullness of God." (3:16-19)

A love that surpasses knowledge? But I am not sure that we ever read our Bibles or think about God as someone to have a *love* relationship with.

Royal Husband?

God does not fit in our tiny little boxes. He is untameable. He is tender. In His own words, He describes himself as "The Lord, the Lord, the compassionate and gracious God, slow to anger, abounding in love and faithfulness, maintaining love to thousands and forgiving wickedness, rebellion and sin." (Exodus 34:6-7) This God is unstoppable and altogether mighty. Yet He holds *our tears* in a bottle. I could say "I do" to a royal husband like this. Could you?

If He means what He says: The Bible itself says it is truth. So if God says something, it is pretty safe to assume He means it. It's not like God lies or something. In fact, He cannot lie. It's impossible. (Hebrews 6:18, Numbers 23:19) The whole point of the Bible is that we might *know* Christ. Not know *about* Him, but know *Him* intimately.

If He thinks I am a beauty: All through the Bible, verses call us beloved, fair one, beautiful, His delight. Not in a collective sense. A specific individual sense. He calls me beautiful. He calls you beautiful. He is enthralled, spellbound, undone.

What do you do with this information?

He is who He says He is. He means what He says. He thinks you are a beauty. Since these three things are true in the eyes of God, a massive mental meltdown has to happen. I found I could no longer fit God's opinion of me in my purse, like lipstick to put on from time to time when I felt a little washed out. I had to undergo a total makeover. The scales had been irreversibly tipped. I had to decide.

Whose opinion matters more?

When I get sucked into somebody else's Hollywood drama, what I am really saying is that the entertainment industry knows more than the God who holds all things together. Hollywood creates air-brushed models, concoctions of body parts assembled on a computer, every flaw removed. God creates Niagara Falls and the reddest rose. He rejoices over us. He knows our every flaw but calls us dearly loved without spot or blemish. Hollywood stirs envy, jealousy, fraud. God satisfies the desires of all things. (Psalm 103)

Can you comprehend how much the God of the universe, the redeemer of all mankind, the beloved Jesus, totally trumps anybody else's opinion on the face of the planet?

For this to sink in though, you have to be clear about *who God is*, and not just who you think He is. He persuaded me. He changed my mind. I began to agree with God.

Jesus was crowned the undefeated Heavy Weight Champion of the World — and of my heart.

When the God who IS comes calling for you — in all fullness, His mind set on glory, His heart bursting with desire — you will never be the same.

Before we move on, I want to say that again. He is who He says He is. He means what He says. He thinks you're a beauty. There is more to your beauty than you have ever imagined. And there is more to your beauty than just your lovely face.

6 — heart beauty

The evil queen would stop at nothing to destroy Snow White. She even took on the disguise of a withered old woman. It's funny that despite her zeal for beauty, she traded it all — her voice, hands, hair, youth and strong back, to destroy Snow White. The irony of this is that now we see her external reality, a conniving old witch, finally matched her internal reality.

Think about the serpent. Of all the shapes God could have decreed, he chose perhaps what best resembled Satan's internal reality.

That's why our words reveal more about our beauty than our make-up. We have all been around the girl who looks good on the outside until she opens her mouth. Wow, the ugliness in her heart spills out and suddenly everyone feels a little sullied.

I was in a department store and saw the three of them. The beauty and her two groupies. She was clearly the ringleader and they hung on her every word because she was turning heads left and right. The more the guys turned to look at her barely clothed body, the louder she got.

"Well I don't need no f---ing boy because all they want to do is f--- me."

Out of the overflow of the heart, the mouth speaks. Her looks may have baited their attention, but her heart and her words cut the line.

Our greatest form of communication is through words. Whether printed or spoken, words have immeasurable weight and consuming presence in our lives. Obviously then there is a beauty (or otherwise) in what we say.

We have all been hurt by others' words and worse, we have hurt others. But instead of seeing this as a battle for our true beauty, we settle for it and rationalize it. Oh that's just life. This is how it works. Look at our culture of sarcasm and satire, disrespect and disdain. We have come to think this is normal. But that is another snake-bite lie.

I wonder if we spend as much time preening and tweezing our hearts as we do our looks? It is a total package. The absurdity of the Total Makeover television show is that they change the surface layer only. What do they do for the heart?

The absurdity of the typical "inner beauty" focus of many Christian churches is that it negates the condition of the temple. God made the body as well as the heart. Changing just the outside or just the inside doesn't cut it. It is a total package. The goal is walking in the image of God. Jesus said He came to bring fullness of life, not just full of looks, not just full of heart, but the fullness of the image of God. (Ephesians 1:23, John 10:10)

Only God is able and willing to create a total makeover, inside and out. He knows the original design for us was to be transformed into the image of Christ.

Buying Time

A cool pair of earrings caught my eye in a store. They were engraved with, "As he thinketh in his heart, so is he." A little dazed, I stood there thinking about what that means. It was one of those God moments when the whole world faded away.

In a flash I went from mindless shopping to a provoking pair of earrings to suddenly doing an inventory about what I *think* about myself. The report card was not good.

I bought the earrings since obviously I needed the reminder.

Funny thing is, I wore them a couple of times before I saw the reference engraved on the back. Proverbs 23:7. For as he thinketh in his heart, so is he. (KJV)

I love how the word of God is living and active, sharper than any two-edged sword. (Hebrews 4:12) At this stage in the Beauty journey I was totally checked out of my own outer component. I had quit. This little pair of earrings began a process of thinking: what do I believe about myself? The short list included: misunderstood, bland looking, sharp-tongued, rude, disliked, unloved, "aggressive", intense and blunt to a fault.

No wonder I was uptight. I will come back to the aggressive comment later. But for now, I will summarize that I was a very high-stress individual. Maybe that is why Jesus said, "Out of the overflow of the heart the mouth speaks." (Matthew 12:34)

But then as the Lord started stripping off the outer beauty lies, He also breathed a whole *new image in my heart*. Was I ever surprised!

I know we are weak creatures. Yes we are human, so we struggle, and we fail sometimes. But there is a power within us, God's power, that is mind-blowing in its ability to change our lives.

My mind was renewed, re-newed, re-made, re-fashioned about the outer me and at the same time my heart was renewed about the inner me. Who would have thought a pair of earrings in combination with God's word could spur on such activity? That's right, God did.

I had been hanging out in Proverbs for a while. A Bible teacher had instructed me to not just read the Bible, but to sit in it, soak in a passage. Ask the Holy Spirit to speak through the passage, I was told. I would read Proverbs over and over, especially chapters 14 and 15. I was confronted about the power of words, wisdom and understanding. I was sharp-witted so the words part came easy. I had that "speaking the truth" part down really well. (Just ask my husband to show you the scars from my lashings.) But I was convicted when Proverbs talked about the words of the wise bringing *healing*. I did not see too much of that in my life.

It was the wisdom, understanding, and especially the speaking the truth *in love* that was sorely lacking. (Ephesians 4:15)

So when the Lord began pouring His love into my life, some of that started spilling out. Out of the overflow of the heart, the mouth speaks. I was amazed at what was coming out, and so was my husband.

A different kind of beauty was being revealed. It had less to do with me getting it right and more to do with Jesus setting me free. The Lord wanted His expression of Jana to be heard as well as seen.

With this rebuilding going on, it was a great gift to come across Colossians 4:6 which says, "Let your conversation be always full of grace and seasoned with salt so that you will know how to answer everyone."

Grace and Salt

What is grace and what is salt?

I asked a room full of high school-aged girls how they would define grace. The room fell totally silent. Awkwardly so.

I laughed a little and realized we needed to back up a bit.

So on behalf of those who are still a little unsure, grace is one of the most important words of the Christian faith. In fact no other religion in the world has anything like it.

Grace comes from God. It is the working of the Spirit of God. It is a gift. Grace is the help we need, the joy we crave, it is the presence of God in our daily lives. It is not a magic genie. It is not eBay®, and it is not Google®.

But just what is grace? It is love, power, sustenance, and

help from the living God. It may sound corny but as a new believer I heard Adrian Rogers define it as:

God's
Riches
At
Christ's
Expense.

Do we deserve it? No. Can we earn it? No. It is God's gift to us because He loves us and wants to help us be who He created us to be. God is so committed to our success, He even gives us the tools necessary to complete whatever He has started in our lives. He gives us undeserved favor and kindness to help us succeed. What is His idea of success? Being transformed to look more like Christ. It is His unstoppable plan. But why that? Because in Christ rested the full glory of God. He was full of grace and truth.

So... what does He have for us if we are to look like Christ?

Glory. Grace. Truth.

God is so committed to this end, He gives us grace to get us there. I love the verse, "And he gives more grace." (James 4) God knows how desperately we need His help. Even when we don't.

As we relate grace to real life, to heart beauty, we see it is God's power through His Spirit to guide our words for His glory.

"Why would God want to help us?" I asked my 8-year-old daughter.

"Well that's a million-dollar question. I don't know," she said.

"Why do I help you Salem?"

"I have never thought about it," she said, looking puzzled.

"Do I have to?" I asked.

"No."

"Then why do I?"

"Because you love me," she said, her eyes wide.

Now put that kind of love at God's perfect level. Does God want to help you live a life of wisdom? Absolutely. Does He want His image, His character, His compassion, His mercy displayed in our words? Absolutely. Can we do that without Him? Absolutely not. Enter Grace.

What is Salt? Salt is medicinal. It has great healing properties. In biblical times when Jesus said, 'You are the salt of the earth,' He was referring to the salt used for treating wounds. He could have said, 'You are the medicine for the earth.'

Salt is also a flavoring. When you sit at dinner, and put a little salt on your meal it makes it just right. Just a dab, a touch of salt can top off the flavor of the food.

Now, put yourself in a room full of friends and watch the conversation spiral downward. It is becoming malicious or gossip or just negative. You speak a little salt and the whole attitude shifts to something that honors the Lord and makes your own heart feel better. The tongue of the wise brings *healing*, Proverbs says.

There is a delicate balance. Did you ever swim in the ocean and get a mouth full of salt water? Too much salt and you gag. But get just splash or two in your mouth and you get really thirsty. Thirsty for what? Water. The same is true with our words. We can make people thirsty with a touch of flavoring, medicinal salt. Thirsty for what?

Living Water. Jesus offers living water to the hurting, battered, rejected, lonely, lost, hungry, thirsty so they will never be thirsty again.

This sounds tremendous, right? But how do we do that? How do we give out— or is that live out grace and salt?

"Let your conversation be *always full* of grace and seasoned with salt."

Here are two ideas that go together like bread and butter. Out of the overflow and always full...

I don't know about you but I leak. Life can really drain me. People drain me. Heck, I drain me.

So I go to Jesus, spend time with Him, worship Him

and let Him love me. When I am with Him, He fills me. The more I am with Him, the more He fills me. And since there is a whole lot more of Him than I can hold, He spills out. Overflows.

I hide His Word in my heart so that His words will pour out. My conversations can't be full of Jesus if I'm not full of Jesus. Now, does that mean, some kind of church-lady-holy-sounding gibberish? 'Bless you sister as thou does bless the Lord in thine act of laundry?' Gag.

You know sometimes when we hear "full of Jesus" we think, "oh full of religion." Or "full of church talk." When we do that it indicates we don't get how cool Jesus really is. When He walked this earth, people wanted to be with Him. All kinds of people. Broken people. Thirsty people.

We go to Jesus so that we will look and sound like Him. But here is a reality check. Have you ever noticed that it is not always easy "to go to Jesus?" It feels like there is a big hurdle. The hurdle comes when we get this faulty idea about God. Instead of thinking rightly about Him, we focus on ourselves:

"I am so bad."

"I just blew it."

"I can't go to Him until I _____" (fill in the blank).

"I have get my chores done so he'll think I am a good Christian girl."

I don't go to Jesus because I have it all together. I go to Jesus because I don't have it all together. The more I know Him, the more I know me. I spend time with Him to find out who I am, to let His Spirit flow through me. I have to be with Him. I want to be with Him. He is what changes my life, and yours, regardless of what has happened in the past, regardless of what the future holds. My heart is full with Him, and this is what pours out of my life. What pours out of your heart?

"Out of the overflow of the heart, the mouth speaks." (Matthew 12:34)

What pours out is what blesses or hurts our friends and families, what blesses or hurts Jesus, and what blesses or hurts ourselves. We all blow it sometimes. But the Lord wants to walk with us and help us grow up in Him. It is a journey. He is ever patient. His mercies are new every morning. He is abounding in love.

Take a minute to give yourself a little test:

Yes	No	
___	___	I speak the truth in love
___	___	I thank God for all things
___	___	I am at peace with all men (and my girlfriends)
___	___	I love my neighbor as myself

Since "an honest answer is like a kiss on the lips." (Proverbs 24:26) you might as well come clean.

Unless you scored perfectly, you might see that you are in need of grace yourself. But take heart. It is an amazing God cycle. I go to Jesus to get grace. Someone hurts me and needs grace. I give grace. I blow it and need grace. So I go to Jesus to get grace. On and on it goes.

He never quits, never relents, never gets discouraged. Isn't God the coolest?

Where are You?

Now lets take the thought about what the mouth speaks and add another verse, "Love your neighbor as you love yourself." (Mark 12:31)

So many times we see this verse and we think about our neighbor. But before we go there let's look at the part about "As you love yourself."

The neighbor doesn't come first.

You do.

You can't love your neighbor if you don't love yourself. Do you love yourself? What do you say about yourself?

What do *you* say to *yourself*... Because it is out of that
overflow that you love others. In fact, how you love your
neighbor is a pretty great indicator of how you love yourself. Ouch. Let's keep digging. How exactly do you learn
to love yourself?

(Hint: The King is enthralled with your beauty.)

You let His love pour in. He shows you who you are.
That is what pours out on your neighbor. And just who is
our neighbor?

When I saw Melissa, I hated her immediately.

She was singing in the choir and she had this giant
bow in her hair. Christian or not, this chick really bugged
me. You can imagine my glee when we ended up in the
same Sunday School class. Oh goodie.

I kept my distance and mocked her. From the back of
the class, I listened to her proper church answers. She
would flail her perfectly polished nails in the air as she
talked. And she used a lot of words. Ugh. What a girlie
girl.

Unknown to me, she was also thinking negative
thoughts about me. Jana is so hard. She is so tough. She
scares me.

Then one day we were sharing parts of our story in a
girls only time. I got to hear her heart and she heard mine.
We had been through some of the same trenches. We were
carrying some of the same scars from college. In a moment, we realized that our hearts had a lot in common
even if our hairstyles did not.

We've been friends ever since. Even though we are still
as different as night and day, we have learned to "love our
neighbor."

The person who dresses funny, who talks differently,
who is unsaved, who you like, who you don't like, these
are all your neighbors. No cookie-cutters, remember? We
are not trying to be identical little shapes perfectly alike.
We are trying to get to the place to see people as creative,
diverse, multifaceted expressions of God the Father.

Romans 13 says "Love does no harm to its neighbor,"

so to reveal our true beauty total package…we love. Not with our love, but God's love.

We give grace because we are all changing. We are all learning how to walk with God. Relax. Take yourself and your friends off the hook. We are all in process.

Here is a great exercise. I learned it from my friend Betsy, who is also very different from me. I was really mad at my husband, Chuck. We were in a crisis season and I was venting and fuming. The overflow was pretty toxic.

She very gently interrupted. She said, "You know Jana, the Bible says whatsoever things are true, lovely and praiseworthy, think on these things."

I was suddenly silent. Talk about speaking the truth in love. Betsy gave me God's truth but it was medicinal salt, not a gagging mouthful. She was totally full of grace, and it spilled over on me.

I got off the phone with her. I needed to be with Jesus instead. I confessed being upset with Chuck but God didn't let me stop there. He is more committed to my success than I am, so He took me to the next level. The Lord led me in a prayer of replacing lies with the truth.

Out loud, I began praying and reading the verse Betsy had given me Philippians 4:8:

Lord, whatever is true about Chuck,
whatever is noble about Chuck,
whatever is right about Chuck
whatever is pure about Chuck
whatever is lovely about Chuck
whatever is admirable about Chuck
if anything is excellent or praiseworthy about Chuck
I choose to think about such things…

And you know what happened? The Lord kept His promise. At the end of that passage is a promise.

"... and the God of peace will be with you." He was with me. He gave His peace. When I turned my face toward Him, He poured grace on both Chuck and me. It wasn't Happyland in a moment, but it was a turning point for us.

Next time you get in conversations or you start running the trash about other people in your head, try that exercise. Let the Lord use your tongue of the wise to bring healing.

The next time you start running trash about you in your head, try that exercise...

Heart beauty can be summed up from this passage in Proverbs 31:

> *She is clothed with strength and dignity. She can laugh at the days to come. She speaks with wisdom and faithful instruction is on her tongue.*
> *(vs. 25-26)*

Oh Lord that the beauty of your words would be found on our lips and in our hearts.

7 — body beauty

Remember Snow White?

There is a classic scene of Snow White scrubbing the courtyard steps and singing with doves. It is a really sweet scene, especially when the prince on a white horse hears her singing outside the garden wall. He stops and scales the wall only to begin *singing to her!* She runs away, embarrassed. But then she looks out over the balcony and listens to his profession of undying love. Her response is to kiss a dove who flies down to the prince. The dove blushes and then delivers the kiss.

Go ahead. Sigh. If you want you can say "aaaaawh."

Without fail every time I show that scene to a gathering of females, young and old, that is what everyone in the room does, sigh and aaaaawh. Even the women who have been jaded by the world pause and revel in the moment.

Do you know why?

Because it is raise-the-roof romantic, that's why. It hits about a hundred of our woman buttons. Snow White is waiting to be "discovered" by her one true love. The prince is strong and smitten by her. Plus he's a great singer. But above all he is speaking straight into her soul… "One love, I have but one love only for you." She is chosen, valued, adored.

Regardless of our present reality this scene triggers emotions deep within us. It arouses the hope and longing for beauty, strength, and romance. And it doesn't matter whether we are "waiting," already taken, or already wounded. These buttons were installed on our hard drive. It is part of our Operating System. Think original design. So the aaaaawhs flow from a place deep, deep down. It's not only natural, it's *supernatural*.

I love Disney movies. Cinderella, Belle, Sleeping Beauty. What babes. All of them were rescued by their heros from great villains, the wicked stepmother, Gaston, Malefi-cent, who were trying to keep them apart. The villains all hated the possibility of true love so much they would do anything to keep the lovers apart. Reminds me of another snake-eyed villain who came to kill, steal and destroy. (John 10:10)

In fact, at one point when the prince singing to Snow White, you see the evil queen watching from a distant window. She is taking in every detail, riveted to the magic of the moment: tender and lovely Snow White, the devoted and pursuing prince, the complete adoration between the two. The evil queen's eyes narrow, filled with contempt and venom. She is enraged.

Sound familiar? The evil one's eyes narrow with rage. He will stop at nothing to keep the Beauty and the Warrior apart. And sometimes he uses their own gifts of beauty and strength as the weapons of destruction.

Let me explain. You know the Disney beauties we just talked about? What makes those stories so appealing and compelling is the innocence and unselfish devotion be-tween the two lovers. It is the "exclusive" nature of their love. The First Kiss. The True Love. This is not random relationships. It is the "forsaking all others" element that makes their love so priceless.

You may think I am exaggerating. Try this on. The prince has just awakened Snow White with a loving kiss. Her eye-lids flutter as does her heartbeat. They look at each other with pure adoration. Then — Snow White confesses that she has already slept with each of the seven dwarves.

Talk about a downer. How do you think the prince would have reacted to this? Did Cinderella lose anything but her shoe at the ball? Did Belle do the nasty with the

Beast? Did Sleeping Beauty get tired of waiting on Prince Phillip and get it on with the royal guard?

Do those questions sound sacrilegious? We recoil at the baseness of the suggestions. But why?

We recoil at the suggestion of scandal because these are pure and untainted love stories. It is not their perfection that attracts us, it is their purity and unity. They have complete one-hearted devotion for each other.

We witness the perfect dance of their strength and beauty, the fitting together and the hum of it is so strong that both of them are better, more, enhanced by their union.

The idea of it, Beauty and Warrior in complete harmony in a beautiful garden, strikes a deep chord within us. To cheapen the idea with heartless sex with "outsiders" is to mar the fabric of the story that so touches our souls. You see these are not just Disney stories. They are God stories.

How much more then do outsiders mar our own love story?

If you are younger, there is a measure of hope when you think about your own love story. It is likely still being written. You are still eagerly waiting for your prince.

But if you are older, the mention of purity, unity, your love story — may bring up shame, heartache, abuse, neglect, divorce. I think of the young woman I saw recently at the store who was wearing a t-shirt with three words printed on it: Jerks love me. That is pregnant with meaning and doesn't sound much like a fairy tale, or at least not one with a happy ending. We feel like we were picked off. We got ripped off. We got kicked out of the garden.

If that's true of your story so far, the coming chapters will offer a healing salve to soothe your aching need for restored glory. But regardless of your age or situation, let's address the need for a whole new definition of body beauty.

Our belief in our own worth and value is critical to

our hearts. Naturally, the battle is fierce about who and what to believe about our worth. We live in a culture that openly mocks the very thing we love in fairy tales: beauty, strength, unity, purity. We all want to be a woman worth fighting for, just like the Disney Beauties.

But we hardly dare to hope for being *treasured*.

Why?

Because in today's society "forsaking all others" is a passing fancy before and after marriage. It is outdated, old-fashioned.

It is ridiculous. Almost absurd. Society tells us women are commodities, something to be consumed by many men, rather than to be chosen and treasured by only one.

I was forwarded a random email in which the originator dared to confront the perspective of how women today are presented as "sexual urinals" in our MTV culture. Beautiful female bodies whose sole function is to just hang around and be available for whenever there is an urge for some male release. This goes against every code and fabric of our feminine hearts. The problem is that, when everything is free game nothing is worth fighting for, much less dying for.

So here we are. We are forced to live in a cultural Gaza strip, the dangerous land between the reality of our culture and the hope of a fairy tale connection. The ache in our hearts is about as broad as the horizon. And it used to make me really, really mad.

I was so "anti-fairy tale" that I was going to write a book called *Happily Ever After, Isn't*. Do you hear the bitterness? It is out of the overflow of a heart that was one of the Beauty War casualties.

8 — dark days

I started having sex when I was 15, one month away from my 16th birthday. I thought I was ready. (Have you heard that before? It's crazy when girls use that line. Ready for what? Rejection, heartache, pregnancy, STD, what exactly were we ready for?) But I thought because I loved him and he really wanted to be "with me," that somehow that added up to a good equation.

Anyway, he seemed special. He made me feel special. And in my world, feeling special counted for a lot. Marriage didn't really enter my picture, because I didn't want to get married. It's ironic how I always needed a boyfriend but I made up some fantasy about not getting married. I would attach myself to a guy who met the "you're special" need but at the same time adamantly insist that I didn't need a guy. Go figure. If I'm honest, I did want a guy but didn't think I was good enough to get the kind of guy I longed for.

So I traded my virginity for feeling special. That boyfriend lasted about six months with three sexual encounters. That's how long it took for me to find out that he had been sleeping with another girl at a different high school. As if the betrayal wasn't hard enough to deal with, he accused me of not really being a virgin. He acted like his unfaithfulness didn't really matter anyway, since he thought I really wasn't so "special" after all. I gave all I had. He threw it on the ground and trampled it.

He was a pig. I was a fool.

I wish I had learned my lesson then, but I did not.

Instead, over the years, there were several boyfriends. Each time I would ask in my heart, 'is he the one who will really love me?' A lot of those times I would give my love in the form of sex. Every time they gladly took the sex but never took or gave love. Over time there was a disconnect with my heart and my body. I remember consciously trying to beat the boys at the sex game. They want to play with sex, I can do that too. Only in my mind I would conjure up some happy ending that I would also win their heart. I would be the one who captured their attention and their love. If I looked good enough, felt good enough, I would win in the end. But just like the beauty pageants, I got no first-places ribbons.

It seemed like most of them walked away unharmed.

I got an STD at 17, pregnant at 19 and viral STD at 24.

History Lesson

I used to think I was the only stupid one when it came to sex. But there are scads of us out there. And we are hurt and bitter and wounded. Sure we were the ones to lay down. We were the ones saying we were "ready."

But the one thing we didn't get was truth. Truth about who we are. I don't mean truth according to Hollywood, I mean real Truth. Capital "T" Truth. Truth about what the goal is, truth about why our hearts kept looking for something, someone, to fill the ache, the longing, the void. The truth about what it would cost.

The one thing I share with every woman who has thrown away her virginity is — regret. There has never been a time, not one single time, after hearing my story that a young woman has come up to me and said, "You know I am so glad I gave my virginity away for nothing. It was worth all the pain." Never once.

We know better. The truth is too painful to deny.

We were willing to trade something right and noble and true for a few moments of fun or "romance" or whatever name we called it. But our little thrills in no way equaled what we could have experienced had we loved ourselves more than we loved our boyfriends. We just didn't not understand how glorious sex could be if you are doing it God's way. Otherwise, we would never have been so easily duped.

How did we as women get where we are today? I look at the coming generations and it is disturbing. It was a war zone when I was in high school.

Today it looks like a nuclear bomb has gone off. We are so out of control. And even in this the Lord is not surprised.

> *"But you trusted in your beauty and used your fame to become a prostitute. You lavished your favors on anyone who passed by and your beauty became his." (Ezekiel 16:15)*

Sound crazy? Your beauty became his. Watch how we lose part of who we are. Let's talk about dress codes. Remember the season of thongs combined with low rider jeans? It was the unwritten fashion code of the day. Girls were sitting down showing everything God gave them and yet they failed to understand why the guys were on full hormonal alert! I was at a church during this fashion season and a young woman went to the front to pray. She knelt down and I think every male in the church just about passed out. Praise the Lord that she was bowing before God. But it was a sad illustration of how the battle rages on, both in and out of the church.

For the sake of history, I want to give you a brief walk through time. In the 1900's somebody came up with the idea of a Uni-bra, a corset that would squeeze your breasts together so it would look like one big breast. Huh? In the 1920's, the flappers first showed *calves* and *ankles* to the scandal of all. The 1960's hippies introduced mini-skirts. Don't forget about the 1970's with hot pants and the 1980's yuppies with long skirts slit up to their wazoo.

And today the X and Y generations sport sheer gauze

tops, bare bellies, and mini-minis. In fashion we keep showing more and more. But in relationships, we keep getting less and less. Does anybody else hear that hissing?

9 — gold rings

Before I met Truth, I would hear the Scripture, "Like a gold ring in a pig's snout, is a beautiful woman who shows no discretion." (Proverbs 11:22.)

I would just scratch my head. Try as I might, I could never really get the meaning of that verse. How on earth did that matter to me in real life terms? I wanted to be beautiful. I wanted to dress so that I looked beautiful. I wanted to turn heads. Why would God be such prude?

At the True Beauty boot camps I see similar confusion when I put the verse on the screen.

Let me break it down. Have you ever seen a pig? Not the cute pink ones. The big fat ones with muck on their feet and faces. The ones with hair on their noses, the nasty looking ones. Now imagine a beautiful shiny ring of gold. Custom designed, hand-melded by the finest craftsman. One of a kind. Now, see this priceless gold ring stuck in the hairy nose of one of those big fat pigs. Imagine the pig pawing at its nose trying to eat that ring, because as far as the pig is concerned, the ring is like everything else in its life — something to eat, to consume.

It might as well be a overripe banana or a molded loaf of bread. It is just something to fill its belly. The pig has no concept or understanding of pure gold.

But someone had to put that gold ring in the pig's nose. In essence, someone just threw that gold ring away, discarding its value and worth.

Now, how does this relate to the beautiful woman?

You see it all the time, a woman just throwing her beauty around for public consumption. Take singer Beyonce'. At one recent MTV award ceremony she had on a flashy gold top that was unbuttoned to the waist and gaping open. It gaped open so much that she dared not lean over to shake her fans' hands for fear she would fall out altogether.

Go to the grocery store to feast your eyes on the gamut of cleavage and flesh in the star magazines. Lots of gold rings thrown out for pig-like consumption and getting pig-like appreciation in return. Snort, snort, grunt.

Another story that would be comical if it didn't make you want to throw up is about Cindy Crawford, the icon of American beauty, at least for a while. She posed nude in *Playboy* magazine. She was reported to have been pleased at how she measured up in the glossy double spread. But the same article said that she was startled and "disturbed" when she found out middle- and high-school aged boys looked at her pictures and masturbated. "I had no idea," she said, shocked.

Really Cindy? What exactly did you think those pictures were for — art?

"Like a gold ring in a pig's snout, is a beautiful woman who shows no discretion." (Proverbs 11:22.)

This is how women throw their beauty away. They put it out there for pigs to feed on. The pigs root around and wallow in their exquisite beauty, and then walk away. But women can't understand why the pigs don't appreciate them.

What does Jesus mean when he says in Matthew 7:6 "cast not your pearls before swine"? Why does Jesus warn us? Because he knows the pigs will do what? Turn and rend you. Tear you. Hurt you. Reject and wound you.

Am I saying all guys are pigs? No.

But women who don't know they are pearls most ofen attract men with pig-like qualities. Women who don't know they are pearls keep casting themselves out for guys to feed on. Then these precious pearls are wounded deeply. Can you see how neither pig nor pearl is living out of the

10 — the horizon

Who are we anyway? Who are we becoming? What are we shooting for? If you are a middle school-aged girl you want to be like high school-aged girls. If you are in high school you want to be like college women. If you are a college woman you are looking at the newly married wife with her home and her man and babies on the way.

But a funny thing happens. We don't keep looking forward. There is a day when you look in the mirror and you think "Where did I go?" There is this weird moment when you start looking back. The thirty-somethings look back to their pre-baby twenty-year-old bodies. The forty-somethings look at pictures of when they were thirty and think, "Man I looked pretty good!" And the fifty-somethings look back and say, "Hey I remember when my breasts used to be up here."

Do you see how looking forward or backward distracts from the fact that there is MORE to us than that? I have pictures of myself big and small. No matter the size I was, I remember hating the way I looked *at the time*. I have friends who won't let you take their picture at all.

After I taught at one college event, a beautiful girl came up to me and said, "Wow I needed to hear the truth about my beauty. I just wish my mom could have heard it. She is fifty years old and all she thinks about is how she looks. It is so sad. She is so insecure."

At 50, she is still asking "mirror, mirror...?"

What a legacy this mother has passed down.

So the hard questions follow: what legacy are we living under? What legacy are we handing down to not only to our daughters, but to every woman we know?

Isn't it time to say, 'Enough!'?

We are already becoming someone. Someone's wife. Someone's mother. Someone's friend. But are we becoming women of Glory? That is God's goal for us. Restored Glory.

You don't get restored glory by throwing away your beauty to every guy that passes by. We are more than gold rings in a pig's snout.

How Far?

'Kaylie' said she kissed a boy. I asked her, "Why?" "It was his birthday, I had to give him something." She is eight years old.

An article in one of the gag-me girl magazines tells how a girl was a victim of a peeping tom. "He looked up my skirt!" screamed the headline. But when you look closely at the photo, her skirt was about two inches below her crotch.

My question was, "What skirt?" The girl had gone way too far and then cried foul play. I would like to call foul play on us as women sometimes.

I often ask my female audience, "Do you like catching a guy's eye?"

"Yeah sure!" is the animated response. Do you like it when you're with your guy and some other girl catches his eye? Same emphatic response but this time the answer is — "No!"

Then I lay down the gauntlet. "Okay, say you are married and you want to be the desire of his heart, remember Snow White? And then some chick comes along half-naked and pulls him away from you. How would you feel?"

The moment of revelation is priceless.

The age of the woman isn't the issue. The beauty thrown out is the issue.

Inevitably one or two girls criticize the guys being gross.

I really address the guys' need for self-discipline. But I bring it back to why do we do what we do as women?

How far is too far? How old were you when you first started thinking about this question?

It is one of the top questions from middle-, high-school and even college-aged girls. This includes the "good" girls. They want to know how much they can, or must, give away.

I flip the question. It is not how much you give, but how much of your beauty will you save? If you give kisses at eight because of a birthday, what will you give at 15, 17, 19, 25 when he is all over you and "really needs it"?

We want to be treated like the Beauty, but we don't want to preserve, protect, defend or honor our bodies.

Here's the rub: if we won't respect ourselves, why should the guys?

We seem to have a hard time understanding we are gold rings and pearls. We seem to have a hard time telling the princes from the pigs. Our hearts long for the prince, but we settle for having our bodies consumed by the pigs. After all, a warm, *temporarily attentive* pig is better than no guy at all. Right?

Why are we tempted to just throw our beauty out for any passing guy to enjoy? I think we do because if you hear a lie loud enough and long enough you will believe it is true. We have been told over and over to use our beauty to snag a guy. But this is a lie.

Of course there is mutual attraction between the sexes. God meant for man and woman to delight in each other. But not for every man to delight in every woman! We throw our beauty out for anyone who will look.

There's just one little hitch. Today's guy is a little more satiated than past generations. Where Grandpaw used to get a thrill from seeing ankles, today's guy has hundreds of scantily clad bodies to cruise, not to mention instant access to internet babes. With this pressure, we're tempted to think we need a little leverage, a little something extra, to make us stand out in the crowd. So we throw a little cleavage here, a little belly there. Some thigh, some ass. No problem. You want to see more? Okay, here's my thong.

Stop. Before you protest and say 'not me', let me remind you of the super tight shirts and super tight pants that grace our schools and churches. We don't seem to know how to be appropriately clothed and still feel beautiful.

The 'how far is too far' question first pops up as we stand in front of our closet trying to dress for school, work or church. All this fashion dilemma happens before the boyfriend.

The real pressure point of the 'how far is too far' question comes after we get a boyfriend. If we show all the goods to attract someone, when a boyfriend does come in for the kill we don't have a lot of wiggle room left.

The scenario usually goes like this: She showed it. He has seen it. She's glad he likes it. He wants it. But now what? He demands. She relents. He wants more of what he's seen. She relents. He throws some love words around the touching and she relents all the more, thinking somehow she is being a woman. Deep in her heart is the cry of the Beauty, but her body is covered in pig slop.

Have you ever felt like you were stuck in this hopeless cycle?

It's called shame. When you start to get tingles of "something's not right here," or "why do I feel so bad" your heart has triggered an alarm system. Whatever you were doing, your heart has protested that the activity is hurting you. It caused you to feel dishonored, compromised, degraded. This is when guilt or healthy shame is good. It helps us navigate our decisions.

We have a choice to respond to the alarms, to discontinue the harmful behavior. But we can also choose to ignore the sirens.

When we ignore the sirens, that's when shame turns destructive. Because eventually instead of believing that you have *done* something bad or harmful, and feeling badly, you come to believe that you *are* bad. And when you believe you are bad, the next phase is hopelessness.

Most often this hopelessness is expressed in phrases like, "It's too late for me," or "What does it matter now?" or

"Who cares anyway?" This is why women of all ages continue to misuse their beauty and their hearts even though they have been hurt numerous times. They have lost hope that they will ever be good enough for anything better.

What would happen if we actually equipped our own hearts, and our daughters' hearts, with the truth about who we are — gold rings and great pearls. What if we taught them how to be "High Towers."

What is a high tower? It is a protected place where the treasure is stored. No one lets a treasure just sit out in broad daylight to be picked over and stolen piece by piece. It has such value that it is under lock and key and guarded at all times.

Go back to the Disney beauties. Most of them were hidden away, locked away, or stolen away. They were not leftovers or community property. They were not shared at all. They were rare jewels, pearls, and thus were worth every effort required to get them.

But today a high tower philosophy sounds boring. No adventure, no fun. We seem to confuse being prized with being a prude. A woman will advertise with her body the belief she holds in her heart. Whether she be a harlot or a heroine.

Oh how we want to be valued, fought for, come for, rescued. But just like Eve, we use our beauty and take matters in our own hands. The same doubt of "did God really say" that echoes in our ears.

Did God really say that He would provide a husband?
Did God really say that the marriage bed was to be honored by all?
Did God really tell us to hide our treasure?
When it comes to love, can we really trust Him after all?
Does it have to be marriage?
Can we just settle for messing around?
The woman trusted her beauty over her Maker.
Can you hear the hiss of our culture?

Too Far...

I told a friend of mine the other day that we are the most sex-saturated country in the world yet we know nothing about sex, let alone intimacy or love. The world trains our women to do whatever it takes to get attention. Then marriage comes along and the world (and even the church) tells wives to do whatever it takes to keep his attention.

When we have no boundaries before marriage, meaning we have already had many sexual encounters, it makes marriage all the harder.

If you don't know how to have healthy boundaries with a guy you hardly know, how will you have healthy boundaries with the guy you are married to whom you really want to please? It is about you understanding and guarding your honor. Even in marriage.

This is an R-rated point, but a common question among newlywed wives is, do I have to have "____" sex? We don't like to talk about sex and use words like oral, anal, this position or that. But our women are under attack, even women in the church. The common response is that within marriage "anything goes."

But I beg to differ.

Hebrews 13:4 says that "Marriage should be honored by all, and the marriage bed kept pure." Do we view the marriage bed as holy at all?

When women ask me "do I have to..." with their husbands, I ask them where that sexual suggestion came from. Is it because the couple was sexually active before marriage and they are trying to find something new? Is he pressuring her because he saw it somewhere else? Pornography has placed an inordinate amount of pressure on women to "perform" certain sexual acts so that their husbands can duplicate what they have seen in less than holy places.

Some things, like anal sex, come from the idea that a woman is to be consumed, regardless of the shame and pain it might cost her. Can you see the link between giving away our beauty and getting stuck in the marriage bed? Both stem from a wrong definition of a woman and her purpose.

When a woman doesn't know her value, she won't know how to defend it. She will get caught between her heart and the man's desire every time until she lifts up her head and says, that's not what I was created for.

Just for the record, anal sex goes against every medical indication of what this body part was created for. Not only is it painful, it is dangerous and degrading. Do you think the Lord cares about this?

Of all the *many* freedoms He invites us to *enjoy* regarding marital sex, He blatantly says in multiple places that sodomy is an abomination. That's pretty strong language.

Here is my rebuttal. I invite women to pose three questions to their husbands should such requests be made of them:

Would you like it if someone inserted a broom in your bottom?

Do you want it bad enough to make me physically sick?

Would you like someone doing this to your daughter?

To bridge the gap, I challenge that if you don't want someone doing this to your daughter, why would you feel the freedom to do it to your coheir in Christ?

Does this sound outrageous? Before you dismiss it, talk to the woman who had to have reconstructive surgery from this unwanted practice with her husband. Or listen to the young bride who simply does not know how to tell her husband that she feels raped by his favorite "position."

I read an *Glamour* article about Ariel Levy who has studied the female identity shift in past and present generations. Her book is called *Female Chauvinist Pigs*. In this interview she remarked that when we embrace the current porn image of a woman, it is as off-target as the 1950's housewife stuck in the kitchen. She goes further to say that if we're "imitating strippers or porn stars — women whose job it is to imitate actual female pleasure — then [we're] imitating an imitation. It's a performance. The result is a total lack of emphasis on personal desire."

I would go one step further and say it is a total lack of the unity, exclusivity, and untainted love that so touches our hearts in the Disney movies.

This is not what God was up to when He created men and women. He had a different plan. "The man and woman were both naked and they felt no shame."

Can you even imagine what that's like?

No shame. What a concept.

I looked up the definition of "shame." It means dishonor. They were both naked and there was no dishonor. No honor had been taken away from the man or the woman. They both stood fully exposed, fully seen by the other, and they fully honored the other. On top of this, it was just the two of them. Not the two of them and memories of several other lovers. Remember Snow White and the Prince? It is the exclusivity and the wholeness of just two people entering a sacred place together. Talk about a fairy tale.

11 — blessings and curses

Proverbs 5 is a knock-down, straight to the point passage about blessings and curses of sexual purity, strength and beauty.

Read it slowly. Carefully. Look for yourself in it.

> *Warning Against Adultery*
> *My son, pay attention to my wisdom,*
> *listen well to my words of insight,*
> *that you may maintain discretion*
> *and your lips may preserve knowledge.*
> *For the lips of an adulteress drip honey,*
> *and her speech is smoother than oil;*
> *but in the end she is bitter as gall,*
> *sharp as a double-edged sword.*
> *Her feet go down to death;*
> *her steps lead straight to the grave.*
> *She gives no thought to the way of life;*
> *her paths are crooked, but she knows it not.*

Take a look around to see the women and men who give no thought to their way of life. It is the same lie as "if it feels good, do it." If it is good for you, then it is good. Much like the song from yesteryear, "if you can't be with the one you love, love the one you're with."

What a lie. No matter how good the beat of the music is, it is still a lie. Cindy Crawford can call her *Playboy* and

Sports Illustrated pictures anything she wants. She, and other women like her, lead men straight to the grave.

Let's keep going.

> *Now then, my sons, [and daughters]*
> *listen to me;*
> *do not turn aside from what I say.*
> *Keep to a path far from her,*
> *do not go near the door of her house,*
> *lest you give your best strength to others*
> *and your years to one who is cruel,*
> *lest strangers feast on your wealth*
> *and your toil enrich another man's house.*

Lest you give your best strength to others. Think poured out for nothing. There is an odd verse in Proverbs 31 that reminds me of this warning. It says, "O my son, O son of my womb, O son of my vows, do not spend your strength on women, your vigor on those who ruin kings." (vs. 2, 3)

Remember the Warrior and his reflection of strength? God is telling him, again and again, "I know women will try to rob your strength. They will use their beauty to seduce you. But resist them, they will sap you." Here is adultery, so beautiful but so very deadly. And for those who refuse to listen to his counsel, the Lord spells it out for them.

> *At the end of your life you will groan,*
> *when your flesh and body are spent.*
> *You will say, "How I hated discipline!*
> *How my heart spurned correction!*
> *I would not obey my teachers*
> *or listen to my instructors.*
> *I have come to the brink of utter ruin*
> *in the midst of the whole assembly."*

Our pastor, Dr. Rick Dunn, once announced the statistics of men in the church who have come to the brink of utter ruin losing their churches, their families, their strength. He said that 40% of all pastors admit to having an extramarital affair since the start of their ministry, 50% of their marriages will end in divorce, and 1500 will leave the ministry each month because of some moral failure.

This is just *pastors.*

Now add to that the diseases, depression, addictions, and divorces due to the other Warriors and Beauties being led astray.

Utter ruin.

The snake's eyes narrow and smile with satisfaction at their downfall.

However. The Lord is all-knowing and all-powerful. He knows what happens when we listen to the hissing of the snake. And in His compassion He warns us of evil but promises us great reward. Instead of utter ruin, He tells us of the fullness of His plan:

> *Drink water from your own cistern,*
> *running water from your own well.*

Now listen to what God says to the woman. This should help shut down any debate about the harmless nature of clothes or lack thereof.

> *Should your springs overflow in the streets,*
> *your streams of water in the public squares?*
> *Let them be yours alone,*
> *never to be shared with strangers.*

I read this passage and my head about popped off. This is a perfect picture of what is happening in our culture today. We share our streams of water, our beauty, with strangers, with anyone in the public squares. But the Lord calls us to a higher place, a greater reward. He knows the plans He has for us. If you want to question God, why don't you question Him about these next lines:

May your fountain be blessed,
and may you rejoice in the wife of your youth.
A loving doe, a graceful deer—
may her breasts satisfy you always,
may you ever be captivated by her love.

I have read these verses out loud and said to the Lord, "I am holding you to your promise. You promised blessing and I am asking you to make good on what you said."

Frankly, it does my heart good to know that God is thinking about breasts.

The guys seem to be particularly relieved also. When I read this passage to a group of young men they find out God not only understands that breasts are very important to them but also that He has *promised them* a pair. This is really big. No pun intended.

God didn't promise many pairs, real or fantasy, He promised one pair in the wife of his youth. His wife. Not his date, his girlfriend, his fiancee, or his live-in. His wife. That word 'wife' translates in Hebrew as Ishshah, my woman. There is that exclusivity thing again. One man, one woman, for life.

Here is the promise. We receive the blessing of the Lord when we treasure our strength and beauty, when we protect and preserve it for the exclusive nature of marriage. When we trust God's timing, his provision, there is blessing.

Just what do the Beauty and the Warrior receive as a blessing?

The woman has the joy of knowing he delights in her beauty but that he is captivated by her *love*. The seasons change but still he rejoices in her just like he did in the beginning. She gets her heart's desire of being delighted in and truly loved for who she is.

And the man? He has been given a Beauty of great price and with her comes the deep satisfaction of his heart and strength. And love. Instead of the utter ruin of the adulteress, where his strength is spent in foolishness and futility, he finds the deep mutual satisfaction of relationship and true intimacy with his Ishshah. He pours out his strength on her to the glory of God. The man gets what he truly wants.

Together, they experience being truly known. Intimacy.

But God is thorough. He wants to be very clear about the blessing and the curse. He calls the man and the woman to look clearly at the choices and the consequences:

> *Why be captivated, my son, by an adulteress?*
> *Why embrace the bosom of another man's*
> *wife?*
> *For a man's ways are in full view of the Lord,*
> *and he examines all his paths.*
> *The evil deeds of a wicked man ensnare him;*
> *the cords of his sin hold him fast.*
> *He will die for lack of discipline,*
> *led astray by his own great folly.*

In my own marriage I have seen the blessing and the curse. I attest that what the Lord promises, He delivers. But let me dig a little deeper. It is a small detail but huge in implication. The Lord had a plan for intimacy in the garden. It was the glory of a man united with the glory of a woman in the presence of the living God. It was to reflect the glory and love of the Father, Son and Holy Spirit.

And that snake Satan may have thought all was lost for the man and woman when they were banished from Eden, but nothing thwarts the plans of God.

Repeat: nothing thwarts the plans of God. He made the Warrior. He made the Beauty. He knows what real strength and real beauty looks like. And when marriage is done well, it always brings Him glory. But you cannot do relationship well, without the Spirit of God.

His plan is that relationships will require Him to reflect Him. We are to live out of a love that is from Him, through Him and to Him. Our utter dependence on Him has been and will always be God's primary goal.

12 — well done

You remember the fairy tale wedding in chapter one with a rose petal path that my daughter and the bride floated down on. There was another moment before the wedding that changed my life. Literally.

As the wedding coordinator, I was bustling around clipboard in hand, checking off the many details with no time to lose. I was looking for a candle lighter in a back room. Got it. Heading back into the mayhem, I walked past the bride's dressing room. All her bridesmaids were standing around the bride in a circle. I stopped short for a moment to absorb what was happening.

Years before, when these girls entered college they also entered a covenant agreement. As part of their initiation into a sorority, they were invited to enter into a ribbon ceremony. If they came forward to have a white ribbon tied around their waist, they were promising to honor their bodies from head-to-toe from that day forward. So serious was this pact, that those who made the vow had the freedom to ask fellow sisters at any time: "Do you still get to wear the ribbon?" Their answer would affect future events.

I was witnessing the culmination of the ceremony.

This beautiful bride, only moments before her wedding celebration, had the same ribbon tied once again around her waist by one of her sisters. This time it was a token of victory. A banner signaling the war is won. This time the ribbon was tied around her waist as an unknown gift for her husband. An external symbol of the internal reality. She was a high tower. She had guarded her treasure, her beauty. Now with complete joy she would let her husband untie her ribbon.

Her college sisters held hands and encircled her. Then they blessed her and prayed for her yet again but this time with thanksgiving that she had withstood the pressures and desires and had held true to her promise of head-to-toe purity. They prayed for God's delight in her marriage and on her wedding night.

As they pulled her gown over her ribbon, Allison laughed with glee. "Matt (her soon-to-be-husband) can take this off later. "

Then she added with a coy smile, "With his teeth."

(The man and the woman were both naked and felt no shame.)

I was astounded. Speechless. Jealous. Delighted. So this is how you do it, I said to myself as tears ran down my face.

What an amazing blessing she gave, not only to her husband, but to herself. What a legacy for her children. And to see the power of women standing together, lifting each other up, together holding back the onslaught of pressure inspired me. It can be done. It is being done. When truth enters the picture, everything changes.

The Bible says, "for them that honour me I will honour" (1 Samuel 2:30, KJV) I have witnessed this truth time and time again. It's the spiritual principle of what you sow, you will reap. When we sow honor and respect for ourselves and for others, it is what we reap. If we don't have very good harvests, maybe we need to go back and look at what seed we sowed.

13 — power of a kiss

There is power in a kiss. Just like in the Disney movies, there is the epiphany, the first kiss that makes our hearts soar. But these were no ordinary kisses given freely to anyone or used as recreation.

No, the Disney kisses meant something. These kisses were like promises of commitment, of things to come. Pure things. Right things. They had great value. The Beauty and the Warrior didn't randomly throw their kisses around with any passer-by; they were placed with power and precision on the chosen one. Snow White, Sleeping Beauty, Beauty and the Beast. Each of them experienced transforming kinds of kisses. I think our hearts long for this kind of connection.

So in that vein, I challenge and encourage couples to heed the wisdom of Song of Solomon that says "do not arouse or awaken love til it so desires." Most couples I know who have regretted their lack of boundaries say their sexual activity began with a passionate kiss.

Be good to each other, I emphasize. Don't stir each other up when there is no freedom to fulfill the desire. Even after engagement, I have called for a "holy distance." Because kisses mean something, they have power.

That's why Joe and Jennifer have such a moving story. It really stretched me. From their own convictions, Joe and Jennifer took that commitment one step further.

They resolved to not kiss but also to not even touch each other until they were married.

Hmmmm, this is a bit extreme, I thought. But I knew and loved their heart for the Lord and for each other. They were both really committed to not causing the other to stumble. Even when they were engaged, they did not touch. Joe handed Jen the box with a ring in it. She put on her own engagement ring.

Their boundaries were in place even at their wedding rehearsal. I was walking them through the process of where to stand, how they would take each other's hand for the giving of the rings, etc. They were like people made of wood. She hardly touched his arm. He held her hand like a limp noodle. Nothing. Finally I pulled them away from the bridal party so we could talk privately.

"Look you guys, I so respect your honor for each other. But you must touch each other. Joe, you have to take her hand and help her up the steps. Jen, you have to put your hand in his so he can put the ring on."

"Miss Jana," Joe interrupted, "Tomorrow we'll be married," he said with a twinkle in his eye. "We have *noooooo* problem touching then." Jen blushed and nodded her head vigorously in agreement.

I smiled and shook my head. "Okay guys, I'm so good with that. But tomorrow, don't forget." It was their turn to laugh. "We won't!" they said eagerly in unison. We finished the rehearsal with a holy distance.

What a difference a day makes.

As the vows progressed, they got closer and closer. So when that moment of the first kiss came, it was better than a Disney movie. It was for real. The whole church cheered and applauded. Well done. Well done.

And to close the gap of the holy distance, Joe swept Jen off her feet. Literally. As they were walking down the aisle, he stopped short and whispered in her ear. She looked at him confused and embarrassed at the interruption of the processional. But then he grabbed her flowing train, swept her up into his arms and carried her the rest of the way down the aisle.

Every woman in the building teared up. My daughters watched in wide-eyed wonder. "Lord," I prayed through my own tears, "bless my daughters with the truth of being a high tower. Bless this couple for their courage. May they fully know the joy of marriage in your presence."

He who honors me, will I honor, remember?

◆◆◆◆◆◆◆◆◆◆

This story is about an ardent groom. He came to my friend, mother of the bride, and asked for her help with only three weeks left before the wedding. I don't know what you know about weddings, but the last thing the mother-of-the bride wants days away from the wedding is another item on her to-do list.

But when she heard the request of her future son-in-law, she could not refuse. "I just want her to feel so treasured," he said. "I want her to feel like a princess…"

The groom had purchased yards of velvet fabric. Purple velvet. For a cape. A long, cascading, spilling onto the floor cape. For his bride. There was so much material the mother had to go to the church to spread it out and cut the pattern.

Finally it was finished. The bride was totally unaware of the gift until the wedding day. As they were preparing to leave, the groom draped this beautiful, luxurious garment around his new wife. A sign of honor, of royalty. A sign that says "I know how priceless this woman is."

And the bride truly acted like a princess. She was lovely, she was pure. She was full of grace. But I think the gripping part of the story is the groom's full understanding; he got it. She is far above rubies. She was the Beauty. He was the Prince.

Every time I tell that story, in my heart I wish someone

would do that for me. I wish someone would value me so much that they would go to that much trouble and then in the public eye, declare my worth. Every time I tell that story, every woman in the place wishes she was the bride, and every man wishes he had thought of it first.

There is something powerful in knowing who we are, and having someone else affirm that.

There is something even more powerful in daring to believe that about ourselves and letting the Lord breathe that affirmation into our souls.

There is something equally as devastating when we don't know who we are. My story is worlds apart from these stories.

14 — poisoned fruit

I was trapped. When I found out I was pregnant at 19, I didn't know about the politics of abortion. I didn't even know about the legalities of abortion. To be honest I didn't even know what the procedure of abortion was. All I knew was that I felt like a cornered animal. I was trapped and I had to do whatever it took to escape.

But where could I turn for help? Although I had been in church my whole life, it offered little solace. God for me was a mostly angry, mad God, who was easily disappointed and very demanding. I had long since given up trying to please Him. So now, caught red-handed in my sin, my only thought was to hide from this distant God.

I was pregnant, ashamed, alone and scared to death. The only people who knew were my boyfriend and my "Christian" roommate who was sleeping with a married man. I was on my own. I had to take care of this problem. Like a trapped animal chews off its own leg to survive, I called an abortion clinic.

When I arrived at the clinic they said I was making a very mature decision. They told me no one would ever know and reassured me that my life would get right back to normal. Those were magic words to me, exactly what I needed to hear. But they were lies. More lies were on the way.

"A lot like menstrual cramps," was their description of what was to happen. They gave me a small white pill to help me relax.

I was one of five girls in a holding room. None of us looked at each other. I couldn't breathe. I honestly had no idea what was about to happen. When it was my turn, I crawled up on the exam bed and began to cry. A nurse stood by the bed and held my hand. She told me it was okay and it would be over in a minute.

Then the doctor came in and began the most painful experience of my life. At first I cried from the shame of being uncovered and violated as he forcefully pushed a tool far up inside me. "To open my cervix" he said. Over and over he rammed the tool deep inside me. But that was only the beginning. I clenched the nurse's hand as a whirring sound began. The doctor inserted another tube and began forcing the tube from side to side. A searing pain shot through my whole body. I tried to pull away but he grabbed my leg and pushed the tube in deeper. It felt like a fire had been lit in my belly and then spread throughout my whole body. I was crying uncontrollably as he pushed and pulled the tube against the inside of my uterus. I hid my face with my free arm. The nurse stood there silently as I gripped her hand tighter and tighter.

Suddenly it was silent, except for my weeping. The doctor pulled down the too-small to sheet and said to the nurse. "I think she wanted this baby."

I looked at the nurse bewildered. It was the first time in the whole process that the word "baby" had been breathed.

"Baby?" I managed to gasp.

With that, he laughed. He slapped my leg and said, "Well, its too late now," and strolled out of the room. He might as well have slapped my face.

As I shuffled out of the clinic, I heard a voice in my head as loud as my pounding heart, "God will never love you now," it hissed.

I believed the voice. I took the bite. And at that moment, the shadow fell dark and long.

15 — the kiss

The evil queen demanded proof of Snow White's death.
Do you remember what she asked for? Snow White's heart.

And when she couldn't get her heart, the queen
concocted another evil, a poisoned apple to trap Snow
White in a deathless sleep.

That's how I lived for years. A deathless sleep. Of course
I didn't look beautiful in a glass coffin. I looked every bit
like the angry, bitter, walking zombie I had become. Not
dead. Not living. Still hiding, ever running. Never hoping.
Never singing. Whipped by my constant companions,
shame, suffering and silence.

But the day finally came that the Prince "who had
searched far and wide" found me. And just like Snow
White awoke with a kiss; I awoke with a kiss from Jesus.

A powerful kiss.

A transforming kiss.

A resurrecting kiss.

I cry every time I think of it.

It had been a dark ten years that yielded a brief marriage
and subsequent divorce, heartache, attempts at college,
travel overseas, and many broken relationships. Anger
boiled in my soul like a cauldron.

I was back in my hometown trying to get my life back in
order.

I had recently married my husband, Chuck, and I had
resumed my going-through-the-motions-church life. No
life. Just motions. But this time on the "church-go-round" I

grew more and more restless and angry. One day I had had enough of the *I don't fit in* saga and instead of going to the scheduled church ladies event, I ran out of the building.

Little did I know I would run straight into the arms of God.

I sat weeping on the steps of a vine-covered gazebo and once again I heard a voice in my head. But this time the voice said, *Tell me your sorrows.*

So I did.

I told Him of all the lies and rejection. All the touches from guys who wanted my body but never wanted my heart. All the hurt I had caused and had experienced. Wasted dreams and wasted years. The guilt, failure and hopelessness. On and on my sad tale went.

Anything else? He said quietly.

Fresh tears sprang to my already red eyes. I had immediate recall of the clinic. The fire-like pain. The laughing doctor. The mutually guilty boyfriend.

"No, there's nothing else," I said like a child trying to hide jelly on her face.

Do you think I don't already know?

"Not that. I can't tell you about that," I mumbled, and covered my face with my hands.

Do you think that when my Son died 2000 years ago that this sin wasn't on the cross?

I stood up and held out my hands in utter defeat and desperation.

Through my tears I choked out, "What do you *want*? What do I have to do? I have joined churches. I have been baptized. Three times! Just tell me. What do you *want*?"

I want the one thing you've never given. I want your heart, Jana, your whole heart.

My arms fell limp to my side.

"I don't have any heart left. It's been hurt too many times."

But instead of walking away, I sat down and picked up my Bible. It opened to a book I had never even seen before.

1st John 4...My eyes read the chapter and froze on verse 18.

Perfect love casts out fear.

I shook my head in despair and tried to choke back the tears. "I have never tasted perfect love in my life," I whispered.

I know. You have never known my love. Will you let me love you? Will you give me your heart?

My heart was a jumble of memories. Of times cursing God, playing church and going through the motions. Of attempts at love that were bitter to recall. I had tried everything. But I realized for the first time I had never tried the right thing.

"Yes." was all I could whisper.

In a flash the darkness lifted off my soul. I drew in a sharp breath, like breathing for the very first time. God's perfect love shattered the lie of never being loved. I fell on my knees half weeping, half laughing with pure joy. The prison door had clanged open. I was free. I really was *alive*. My prince had come for me. How sweet was the kiss of life.

The Journey into Worship

Thank you, thank you, thank you. I think that was my prayer for the first several years after being brought to life. Everything was different. Everywhere I saw how the hand of the Lord had drawn me to Him. I began to thaw out of my frozen emotional state. My heart was finally beginning to understand the Scripture I was reading. I saw the Lord answer prayers and move in mighty ways. This God thing, I was delighted to discover, was really *real*. After all my years of denying and cursing and running, I realized how wrong I had been about Jesus. He really did love me and really did die in my place. All I could say was thank you.

I was so thankful in fact, that once I had received His gift of grace, I proceeded to do everything possible to show Him how thankful I was. In the church I attended, this meant serve, serve, serve.

I was like those funny cartoons where someone was heroically rescued and so the rescued person sticks to the hero like glue hoping to jump on any chance to repay the debt.

I served on every committee. I painted. I taught. I sang in the choir, taught English to internationals, did prayer walks. I wrote plays, dug weeds, cooked chili, set tables. I did vacation Bible school. I even did the nursery. I wanted God to know I was really, really thankful.

And just like in those cartoons, the rescued person becomes kind of obnoxious. Because everyone knows, everyone but the rescuee, that the debt *cannot* be repaid.

My life was radically different. My pre-Jesus friends were shocked at the change in me and in my husband who had also become a Christian. My new Jesus friends were shocked at how far I had to go. But we kept learning and growing every year.

My marriage to Chuck experienced major shifts as we learned how to do life according to God. After years of suffering with infertility, after many tears and prayers, we were literally *gifted* with a child. This is spite of even doctors saying we would not be able to conceive because of both of our sexual histories. Life was amazingly sweet and surprising. It had hard places. Even heartache. But God was truly restoring the years that the locusts had eaten, (Joel 2:25). I never dreamed that He could make this kind of a difference in my life. I was so grateful.

But something was missing. Frankly, I started getting tired. Not tired of the work. Every endeavor was a sweet time of calling on the Lord to give creativity and grace and endurance. He was so rich to provide all my needs.

He was showing me giftings and He was rewriting the hard drive in my brain. We worked on my very rough communication skills; He taught me how to love, and showed me how to live a life for God. I knew He was working in my life. But there was something missing. I couldn't begin to tell you what. But I was…hungry. I had this gnawing that would not go away. An itch that I could not scratch.

I remember going to older Christian friends and saying "I love the Lord with all my heart. I read my Bible. I pray. I know He is with me. But isn't there more than this?"

Sadly, their answer was "You're just not serving enough."

This response sent shock waves through my soul and spirit. In that moment I realized God was taking me somewhere totally different. And it would be a total God thing. I would not be able to predict or plan the journey. I would not be able to work it up from my own desire. It would totally be Him leading, because I had *no idea* where we were going.

16 — worship beauty

A Deeper Call

The invitation came by way of sorrow. I was four months pregnant with our second child. You remember that our first child was a total miracle, against the doctors' predictions. So it was a great surprise to have another baby on the way. At the obstetric visit only two weeks earlier, I had seen the baby rolling and flipping inside my womb via ultrasound.

It is always a wonder to see the hidden life. Every time I would see one of our babies inside the womb it was like I was peeking over God's shoulder as He was knitting together a new creation. A sneak preview of things to come.

But this visit was different. On this visit there was an alarm in the nurse's voice when she couldn't find the baby's heartbeat and there was an unusual rush to get me in the ultrasound room. The lights were dimmed. The probe was inserted and the image appeared. "There it is," I breathed with relief. But the longer my husband and I watched, the more my heart tightened. The little body just lay there, arms and legs still, head laying motionless on the floor of my womb. The only movement was my own chest heaving under the weight of the truth. The baby was dead.

Chuck and I held each other and wept.

We began to tell our friends and family. Some asked why did this happen? After our long journey filled with heartache and healing and abortion and infertility and prayers for our healthy baby, they shook their heads and asked, why this?

But in an act of mercy, the Lord led Chuck and me to ask instead, "What is the Lord up to?" We had a sense of something "other" coming.

I had been a Christian for almost seven years. In that seven years I had been blessed to have a church body that helped me steep in the word of God. I had a dear spiritual sister, Nan Sprouse, who helped me grieve for the child that had died in the abortion clinic. I had gone through years of heartache from infertility. I had been calling out to the Lord for a baby and was finally blessed to have our daughter, Salem, three years earlier. Chuck and I had weathered seasons of feast and famine as we sought to break down the strongholds we had brought into our marriage. Through all this living, God had taught me to move beyond the "Why God?" question to "What are you up to God?"

He had convinced me already that He was good. All the time. So when I went to Him with a dead baby in my belly, I begged Him to show me more of Him. "Show me how to trust you more even in this moment when I hurt so much."

I went and looked up the great passage from Job. The Lord gives and the Lord takes away. Blessed be the name of the Lord. (1:20-22) But for this first time, I read the whole passage. And for the first time, as Paul Harvey says, I read "the rest of the story."

> At this, Job got up and tore his robe and shaved his head. *Then he fell to the ground in worship* and said: "Naked I came from my mother's womb, and naked I will depart.
>
> The Lord gave and the Lord has taken away; may the name of the Lord be praised." *In all this, Job did not sin by charging God with wrongdoing. (italics mine)*

He fell to the ground in worship. This wasn't about singing in the choir. This wasn't about singing solos. This wasn't about contemporary vs traditional songs. This wasn't about anybody but God and Job. Alone. And although I didn't have all the pieces of the puzzle, I had an inkling it was because of the worship that Job was empowered to "not sin by charging God with wrongdoing."

It was in this loss, that my husband and I learned to worship for the first time. Worship became more than the words we sang on Sunday. We learned to pour our hearts out before the One who listens and who always cares. We learned to declare His faithfulness and worth even in sorrow. We wrestled with whether God could be trusted with our dreams and our hearts. To go from the elation of our first child to burying our second child was such a great divide. We had to decide what we believed about God.

In the coming days we clung to God. We waited to see if my body would naturally pass the baby. It did not. So we tightened our grip on God as we went to the hospital to deliver our stillborn. We held his lifeless little body, touching his tiny hands and feet. We named him and had a memorial service for him. Through it all we wept and we worshipped.

We asked the Lord to hear our tearful cries, to give us His perspective. We reminded ourselves of who He is. We praised Him that He did indeed create, through us, another beautiful child. We thanked Him for the grace that carried us through this season. We rejoiced in hope that one day there would be a great family reunion. We worshipped and did not charge God with wrongdoing.

These were the first steps in a deeper journey with God.

We had finally gotten over trying to repay the debt of Jesus's blood. We had been invited to go deeper. Now we dared to go *live the life* that had been redeemed by the blood.

Everything seemed different after that season with the
Lord. I must have looked a lot like an awkward teenager
with a slick college guy. Only the motives were right on
both sides. I discovered personal worship. Singing just to
Him. Singing Scripture with melodies He and I made up
on the fly. I discovered worship CDs that propelled me into
the presence of the Lord. I learned to sit. And laugh. And
cry. And talk. And listen.

I was beginning to have a relationship. Not just to God
the Father, like some formal contractual relationship. Not
just saying thank you for saving me Jesus. But something...
intimate.

I learned that my hip bones still knew how to work.
Only instead of swaying to catch a guy's attention, I was
dancing before the Lord. Just the two of us.

Talk about awkward.

The first time, I had music playing and my spirit was
soaring. It was that overcoming kind of feeling. Being
swept away. I couldn't figure out why I was so frustrated
just standing there in my living room. I recognized the
feeling. It was like when you go out dancing and the
music is loud and you're busting to dance and move to
the rhythm but you have to wait for somebody to ask you.
So you stand there on the side lines and twist and move
and squirm. And when you finally get asked to dance,
you would go under the lights and just disappear. The
bass beats in your chest, your hands and arms arch and
curve and your whole body and mind are immersed in the
moment. Any sense of self is completely lost. Just lost.

So here I am standing in my living room and it's as if
I just stepped out on the dance floor. Oh the freedom.
The joy of dancing without shame or sex or comparison.
Dancing in the beauty of what I believe dancing was
created for — adoration, praise, intimacy.

Then it happened. His strong voice in my heart. "I love
the way you dance." I just stopped. I was not alone on the
dance floor.

I had been asked to dance. I picked up my arms and
began again. It was as powerful as a first kiss. A complete

jumble of emotions. An electrical surge going through every limb. And I was gone, gone, gone. Lost in some eternal moment.

When the song was over I laughed out loud. "Lord, " I said, "Why didn't all those folks who spent years trying to save me from hell, ever tell me about this?"

17 — no magic formula

I offer no "quick easy steps for worship." I always tell the girls at the camps and our small group that there is no magic formula. God is just too big and too creative to be put in a box. But I can tell you that according to the Bible, God loves our worship. Think intense emotions. He craves, enjoys, eats up, delights in our worship.

When I started getting the tiniest taste of true worship, the whole Bible looked different to me. Instead of living off of lists of better-do's and should-do's and ought-to-do's, the Bible stories and characters became more real, more life-like, more like — well, me. Flawed, hurting, weak, needy people who were so utterly changed, empowered, encouraged, so altogether *other*, when they walked with their God. When they worshipped in spirit and truth, as Jesus said. I wanted that. The more I worshipped, the more I wanted of Jesus. The more I wanted of Jesus, the more He poured into me, awakened me, defined me, loved me.

Early in my new journey, I came across the Greek definition of worship: *Proskuneo*...To Kiss toward. To adore. To bow down.

Maybe I am slow on the uptake, but this rocked my world. Remember the Disney kisses? The sighs and aaaaaaahs when the prince or hero or warrior takes the Beauty in his arms, pauses to look right in her eyes, and then oh-so-tenderly yet with fierce determination kisses his lover? Maybe we long for the kiss much more than the man.

Kiss me with the kisses of your mouth...

Who said that? Solomon? Better look again. Song of Solomon is a great resource for marriage and romance. But it is much, much more. The kiss is from Jesus. To us. To me. To you.

Proskuneo. What is worship? To proclaim value, to declare worth. To kiss toward, with the kisses of your mouth.

Now are you understanding the power of a kiss? It is a form of worship.

We will always worship something because God made us for worship. What occupies our mind, and hearts, what do we pour our strength out for? That is what we worship. I had to really take a look at what I adore, what catches my fancy. For a long time I worshipped, bowed down, adored the way I looked. The way others look. It was my occupation, my mental focus, my heart's meditation...

But before you throw all kinds of guilt on yourself if you do the same or similar, there is good news. When I inclined my heart to know the truth, taking tiny little baby steps, frail inconsistent jolted steps, I realized that there was something greater and better to worship than my jean size. Then a God thing happened.

Jesus came to me.

He enlivened Scripture, brought songs on the radio, had friends pray unknowing confirmations. He even spoke through one of my daughter's movies, *Joseph King of Dreams*. In the Bible and in the movie Pharaoh calls Joseph Zaphnath-paaneah. The true definition of this name means revealer of secrets, treasury of the glorious rest, even savior of the world. But in the movie they use the expression, "the God who speaks and He lives." I can't tell you how many times the Lord has brought that very phrase to my heart. He truly is the God who speaks and He lives.

18 — His delight

His pleasure is not in the strength of the horse,
nor his delight in the legs of a man;
the Lord delights in those who fear him,
who put their hope in his unfailing love.
(Psalm 147:10-11)

He delights in those…who hope in His unfailing love.

I used to read that and think of myself. I wanted to trust God more. I would tell myself I need to hope more. Now I read that and focus on *He delights*. What could it possibly mean to have a God who delights in the likes of me?

One of my greatest joys in learning to worship is the slow change in my heart. Worship became a long, tender conversation that we would pick up without skipping a beat. The more I proclaimed and agreed with who God said He was, the more He started telling me who I was. And I would argue with Him. And still do, but He always seems to win.

It was in worship that the whole beauty conversation started. He put His loving finger on the part of my heart that had been long shut down and rejected. Even after salvation, this wing of the mansion was closed.

One day He told me He thought I was beautiful. And I said, "I think you're crazy." And He said, *No really, I do.* And so I said, "You have to, you're God. No fair."

Then He said, *No I mean it. I really think you are beautiful. Just the way you are.*

"Prove it," I said.

He told me to write it down and He would do the rest.

"Fine," I said reluctantly. So I got a yellow Post-It ® note and wrote:

I am beautiful.

He delights in me.

Now be transformed.

Then I taped it to my mirror so I could see it every time I went to the bathroom or got dressed or tweezed my eyebrows or brushed my teeth, or said something ugly about my skin, hair, face, thighs — you get the picture.

Note to self: you should never double-dog dare the God of the universe to do anything. Because He can be a real show-off.

I wrote that note in 2001 when my heart was barely beating in my marriage. Today I have enough God stories to fill ten books. Let's just say the note is still on my mirror and now when He tells me that I am beautiful...I smile and giggle and say, I know, *I know.*

One Song

The Lord your God is with you, He is mighty to save. He will take great delight in you, He will quiet you with his love, He will rejoice over you with singing." (Zephaniah 3:17)

He really does sing over us. And sometimes He even lets us hear it.

I was playing the Snow White and Prince clip I had shown many, many times. It is the scene I told you about when he leaps over the garden wall and sings to her.

But this particular day something different happened. I implored the girls to listen to the words. I emphasized how this song expresses their heart's desire — to be loved by the one true love and not the hottie after their body. Listen to what he says, I told them. This is what we long for ...

One Song
I have but one song
One song
Only for you
One heart
Tenderly beating
Ever entreating
Constant and true

One love
That has possessed me
One love
Thrilling me through

One song
My heart keeps singing
Of one love
Only for you

The girls did indeed sigh and coo. But I was awestruck. This time instead of hearing the prince lovingly call to Snow White, I heard, "Jana, this song is for you. This is how I feel about you." I shook my head and smiled.

Never, never double-dog dare the God of the universe to prove anything ...

19 — rewriting the ending

God has such a sense of humor really. Only God would think to totally re-write my foundational life truths as I am working on one of His favorite occasions, a wedding. We have been so battered and betrayed, divorced and disillusioned that it is easy to lose sight of Him and His plan.

But I found out that God loves weddings. A lot. Marriage is His idea, you see.

By accident, I began the tedious business of being a wedding designer. It started out as a favor for my friend who desperately needed help with her daughter's wedding. Many weddings later, here I was again standing before 30 reception tables that need to be dressed and dolled up in white linen, candles and rose petals.

So how does God change my mind and thus change me? By putting me on the front line. Over and over I see the bride and groom, the vows, the celebration, the hope and promise. Over and over He lets me see how to do it right or wrong: either with Him as the source and the center, or just two kids thinking love and/or sex will hold them together. It was in doing weddings, that the Lord revealed His heart about how much He loves marriage, purity, grace, even creative expressions unique to each couple.

When people ask me how I thought of this clever way, or

that unusual look, I honestly reply, "It was God's idea."

It is a real experience every time because God likes to talk to me during wedding preparations. This particular wedding, I was trying to pray through the stress instead of whining. So as I pulled rose heads off their stems and separated the petals, I recounted the to-do list yet to be done.

"Lord, I am so stressed out. How do I get myself in these situations? There are so many details to a wedding and I just need your help. Please help me with all this stuff —"

And then there was a holy interruption.

You know I am planning a wedding.

I was silenced. "You are?" I ventured timidly, half laughing.

I am a wedding planner myself actually.

"Yes I guess you are." I laughed nervously. "So you understand where I'm coming from, don't you?"

I love weddings, Jana. It is one of my favorite things.

"Yeah I do too really." I said with a happy sigh.

But at my wedding, guess who the bride is?

The petals fell out of my hands. I flushed blood red and began to cry.

"Oh Lord …" I whispered.

The to-do lists fell away and all was quiet in this eternal moment.

Here was my prince.

And He had a robe ready for me, ready to drape on my shoulders, in full view of everyone, saying "Here she is. Isn't she lovely?"

He had given me a glimpse. Just a taste, a foreshadow of

things to come. But it was real. And it was life-changing.

Truth does that.

It changes everything.

He rebuilds a God-view of marriage in the middle of my broken world view.

Part II
The Beast

Who has lied from the beginning and lies still today

To avoid criticism
do nothing, say nothing,
be nothing.
– Elbert Hubbard

Lord, now indeed I find
Thy power and Thine alone,
Can change the leper's spots
And melt the heart of stone.

Jesus paid it all,
All to Him I owe;
Sin had left a crimson stain,
He washed it white as snow.
(From Jesus Paid it All,
by Grape and Hall)

The Beast

From the deepest shadows the serpent approached the Beauty. His heart panged in jealousy as he watched her bask in the sun. She was resplendent. He silently inched toward her and cast a cautious glance at the Warrior who was with her. Strength rippled in the man's stature and manner. The wily enemy shuddered slightly, and was careful to avoid the Warrior's reach.

The afternoon passed and the snake and the Beauty talked. The conversation and trust grew as the shadows grew longer. The woman was like a babe, innocent, trusting. But still the enemy advanced his evil plan. He watched her carefully and rehearsed the strategy in his mind. He had to divert her attention from the tree of life. One misstep and all would be lost, at least lost for him.

He must convince her to take from the tree of knowledge. Somehow he must make her long for something she does not have. But she must want it so much she would take it for herself, take it without seeking the Creator. Somehow he must trick her.

"Did God really say that you could not eat of the tree of knowledge of good and evil?" he asked with a easy yawn.

She pondered the question with a slight tilt of her lovely head. "Yes," she said simply, "and to not even touch it," she added.
The serpent's eyes widened with glee, but he quickly resumed his casual manner. The serpent knew that was not what the Creator had said. His evil ploy was working. The woman was beginning to confuse the truth. Victory was surely at hand. Soon, now, very soon.

Later, as the sun set over the glorious garden the enemy felt a deep satisfaction. He bit his lip in hidden ecstasy as the woman pulled the fruit from the forbidden tree and placed it to her mouth. He closed his evil eyes and enjoyed the sound of the skin of the fruit being broken and the juice pouring down her chin.

With an air of nonchalance, he remarked, "See I told you, you would not die."

The woman was nauseous from the taste in her mouth. But it wasn't the taste of the fruit. It was the taste of … knowledge. She was strangely and keenly aware of — herself. She looked to the Warrior and smiled. But her heart churned and raged. She felt weak for an unknown reason, like she was changing, decaying. She knew now what she could not have known only moments before. She was dying.

With a small laugh the enemy hissed, "Hey, I have an idea. Let's share with the man."

The Beauty was undone and she knew it. But as she looked at the Warrior, still pure, still strong, still eternal. She had to do something to keep them together. What could she do to keep his heart?

The Beauty draped her arm around the Warrior's neck seductively. But for the first time, there was evil in her touch. "Just a bite" she offered. "No harm done with just one bite."

In a fleeting moment, the Warrior remembered his Creator, but the Beauty was so dear to his heart, so near. He had to choose, whom would he try to please, the woman or his Maker.
He closed his eyes, and took a bite.

20 — beauty and the beast

We've spent several chapters beginning to dare to believe that God calls *us* His beauty. We've only *hinted* at the thought of *glory*. Before we go there, we must conquer the Beast that would steal all hope and joy and truth.

There is no graceful transition from the wonder of our beauty to the hideous decay of our culture, rampant with adultery and pornography. Anyone who thinks it's harmless hasn't experienced its damaging wake. I have.

So have some of my dearest friends.

Have you?

If you haven't, this journey I'll share still applies to the primary obstacles in your life. The details may be different, but the God-concepts hold true. I invite you to read this with an open heart and mind, because the same God who brought us through this fire, will be faithful to bring you through the fire you may be in.

What God has shown me in this journey is that He is up to something far greater than I can see. Max Lucado once said that the stars shine brightest in the blackest night and that is certainly true for me. My heart in sharing this part of the story is to give hope to women, (and men) that there is a Deliverer. Jesus does indeed restore the years that the locusts have eaten. (Joel 2)

But I also want to challenge us as women. If you are in the thick of this battle, take heart. We are not as helpless as it feels. If you think you're not involved in the particular "issue," or that it's "his" problem and not yours, don't be deceived. The pornography battle strips our men of manhood and literally eats us alive.

But as an overcomer in this war I can declare that *I know my Redeemer lives*, even in this age of adultery.

I encourage you to brace yourself. These next chapters are neither easy nor pretty. But they are real life. Real life for a lot of us. And we need to know that there is a God who is bigger than real life.

The Report Card

I went through a drug store and my eye caught the cover of *Sports Illustrated*, the swimsuit edition. "Pigs!" I mumbled with disgust as I considered the men who would be so delighted at its arrival. But instantly my heart froze. "Has Chuck seen this? God have mercy on him."

I was surprised by my own reaction. Only a couple of years before I would have seen the magazine and gone off on a mental tangent about something new for Chuck to enjoy behind my back, enraged by the Beast who was ever-present in our marriage. But today, I looked at the beautiful woman and felt compassion. I was able to pray for Chuck's protection from this adulteress woman. Thank you Lord, for progress in baby steps.

Then for some reason, with my stomach in knots, I turned and looked again. Closer this time. "God have mercy – *on me*," I said softly.

My body was paralyzed by the internal explosion. What am I supposed to do with this? I stand here with no make-up, two days past shaving my legs and with a bad hair cut. Even if I correct all of that, how can I measure up to this glossy image of perfection smiling at me? What am I supposed to do with this monster of rejection standing between me and that magazine? And what is every other woman, who is more like me than like her, supposed to do?

The small still voice rang out — *remember who you are.*

21 — facing the beast

Boys will be boys.

I think I have heard that all my life. In fact, I spent a great many of my early years trying be "like the boys" because they seemed to get all the perks. In the end, though, I find after extensive observation being a man does not necessarily equal all the perks. Their strength is both a blessing and a curse.

Boys are different. They think differently, act differently, process differently, love differently, even lust differently. And regardless of whether we are surrounded by good and godly men, or rough and ruthless men, they have some basic wiring that demands attention from us as women. Especially that lust part.

Now more than ever our men have been weakened, gutted, betrayed, and in some senses been emasculated by their own God-given design gone awry. The "lust of the eyes" Jesus called it. (Matthew 5:28) The power of their sex drive now drives them instead into adultery, closet stashes, internet stockpiles, and shame-filled self sex.

That's hardly what happened between the man and woman in the garden. Remember the warning in Proverbs 31? Do not pour your strength out on women and your vigor on those who ruin kings. We see the reality of this ruin all around us.

And what about your man? One of the hardest truths to face in marriage is the reality of infidelity.

Unhindered

The Beast of adultery seems to strike out of nowhere. But really it has been lurking and watching for a long time, waiting for an opportune moment.

We all have stories of couples we know who seem happy and then suddenly, at least suddenly for us, they are in the process of divorce. What happened is not an unfamiliar story anymore; one spouse was cheating on the other.

I know when adultery first impacted our little community we were speechless.

Many couples in our Sunday School class hung out as a group, playing games, laughing, telling stories. Then out of the blue, one of the couples stopped coming. This was a great couple — they were leaders in our Sunday School class and the life of the party. We were shocked to find out that the husband had been cheating on his wife and was filing for divorce.

I was madder than a hornet when I heard the news. "How can this be?" I ranted to my unusually silent husband. "How horrible! What a pig. He's a dog. He's a no good..."

I gave a sinister laugh and declared to my husband, my finger wagging in the air, "You better not even try that with me. I'd hunt you down. I'd make your life so miserable you would *rue* the day you met me."

By now, he was used to my exaggerated responses.

Yet his silence silenced me. He was disturbed.

"We all make mistakes, Jana" he said quietly. Sure, I momentarily agreed with him, but this was unforgivable, inexcusable! They have two small kids. She is beautiful. "What more does he want? What more could he possibly want?" I demanded to know. I hoped that the outrage would camouflage the fear that flooded my heart. What I wasn't saying was that if it could happen to them, what would prevent the same for us?

"What more does he want?" I asked again. There was no answer.

They want *more*, I found out. Men want a lot more *more*. Boys will be boys after all.

This *more* reality became a constant threat for me, like being watched from the shadows. Like a strong scent that hangs in your nostrils long after you are away from the person in the elevator. I just could not shake the growing evidence that the dream or fantasy or illusion of "more" was killing a lot of marriages all around me. The faceless Beast was ever on the prowl.

Wake Up Call for Women

The sexual war we find ourselves in is not a "just a guy thing." It is a human thing. We carry different weapons as men and women. We are wounded in different ways. But the war is not to men alone. As mothers, wives and daughters, and as daughters made in the image of God, we cannot check out on the other half of humanity by dismissing it as just a man thing.

We also can't turn up our noses, close off our hearts and give up on the greater goal of true intimacy.

We cannot pretend the Beast is not there.

But we also cannot fight it.

By fight it, I mean fight in the sense that we think we can swoop in with our motherly oversight, tend to the boo-boo, kiss it, bandage it and all will be well in the world again.

We cannot heal the wounds.

We will be wounded by it.

But God will be faithful to heal His men, and His women as well.

22 — boys will be boys?

I was first exposed to pornography in high school. My guy friends told me to grow up. My girlfriends told me to ignore it. My boyfriend thought I should try it. I was eager to please him, so I did.

We went with another couple in separate cars to a soft porn drive-in. Within a few minutes of the movie starting up, I looked over and saw my friend drape his girlfriend's panties over his rear view mirror. I turned to my boyfriend and said, "Don't even think about it."

We left the drive-in moments later when I was sick to my stomach. Not even knowing why it was so wrong, I was disgusted. I felt cheapened. But more than anything, I felt hopeless, utterly hopeless as a female.

Some confused synapses were firing off in my head. I could not be that kind of woman, did not even want to *do* that or *be* that. But how was I to compete? How do you do this woman thing? Is that the standard? Is that what it takes to satisfy a man?

Of course, as adults, we shake our head in knowing agreement and say, I was not supposed to compete and there is an altogether different definition. But still it was an evil seed planted in my heart.

Years passed, boyfriends, locations, even convictions changed, but porn continued to appear. College guys didn't even attempt to hide the magazines in their bathrooms. Men of all ages would slink into the "family" bookstore where I worked and gaze and drool over the slick images in the *men's* magazines. All this was in plain view, in the same store with classics, Bibles, cute posters with Scriptures, children's books and pornography. All side by side. No problem. Something for everyone, right?

The older women I worked with just shrugged their shoulders and hissed, "Men." As if that was the sum total, the universal explanation of what I was observing.

Another incident occurred a few years later. During the very short season of my first marriage, a group of friends, married and unmarried couples, gathered to play cards. As the evening went along we were promised by the host and hostess that they had a special treat to "top off the evening."

Once they got their kids to bed, the treat was a porn video. "To spice up our sex lives," they said with a sick sort of glee. All the guys hooted and cheered. The women laughed uncomfortably and tried to play along. Then the couples snuggled in for a few hours of — inspiration?

Oddly enough, I had married the same guy from the soft porn drive-in years before. I looked at him defiantly and left immediately, angry and dumbfounded. He caught up with me and we walked home in icy silence. I had that sick feeling again from years before.

I felt trapped and, honestly, like a total outcast. When I said I was leaving they all laughed at me and said I needed to loosen up. They, men and women, patted my then-spouse on the back and said, "too bad."

On the way home, he told me I was just too young. To just blow it off. But that was easier said than done.

Later that year I read editorials on the debate about showing porn movies in theaters on military bases. The readers, many of whom were women, were appalled. But one woman was indignant, calling the other female responders "prudes." She said they should be thankful to be "relieved of duty" for one night while their husbands were at the movies.

My poor brain as a young woman couldn't quite figure out why this was so distorted.

Now I know that she was revealing the depth of hurt in her own marriage. Now I know that she totally underestimated porn. It is not a one night distraction but is often a secret lifestyle. Most studies show that pornography is a habitual and addictive behavior. We're not talking addictive like biting your nails, we're talking emotional bankruptcy.

And I sadly doubt if she knew that the role of a woman is not to merely fulfill a duty, whether in marriage or in fleshful fantasy.

All these insight came years later.

But at the time, as a 20-something young woman, the incident just proved to further nurture the evil seed planted in high school.

In every romantic relationship I have had with a guy, there has been a presence of pornography, or at least the admission of its use before or after the relationship. Because I was sexually active with a couple of these guys, it was a running joke that they didn't "need" it during our relationship. So I concluded this was the mantra of a normal male.

In seasons without females, substitute with imitations.

Why do I tell you all this? Because before coming to Christ, I thought that this was what bad boys do whether they were my bosses or guy friends. It was commonplace, everywhere. But I was a little shocked to find out that God's boys do it too.

The Sad Facts

The hard reality is that cases of sexual addiction, meaning pornography, adultery, and even more deviant behaviors, are almost equal in the church as outside of it.

George Barna, who heads a major Christian research

firm, reported that 90% of college-aged males were already immersed in destructive habitual practices with pornography.

Douglas Weiss, a well-known and respected Christian therapist in the area of sexual addiction, says that the numbers regarding masturbation break down into three primary groups of men: 7% who don't indulge at all, 15-18% who do it for pure physical release without mental damage, and the remaining 75% of men who qualify as addicted to self sex — neurologically, socially, and emotionally. They cannot stop without intervention. What are we to do?

23 — no big deal

After becoming a believer in Christ, the Lord set me on the unlikely path of teaching sexual abstinence until marriage. Out of the devastation of experiencing sex the wrong way, the Lord was giving me a voice about the truth of marriage and intimacy, and the truth about the lure of sex, porn and adultery. So for fourteen years, I waded through the maze of male morals. Each time the team I taught with went into the schools, we hoped to find teachers and coaches who taught their young men discipline. But it was rare to find a single coach or happily married man who would support our philosophy. More often their discipline was reserved only for the sports field. The coaches' cry for pushing hard toward the goal was usually limited to carrying the ball or making the tackle. When it came to off the field activities — well, then (knowing chuckle) boys will be boys.

Many of these older men emphasized the need for self-control and will-power to train for football, which lasted only four short seasons. But they had no concern for training young men for marriage, which lasts a lifetime.

If an older man spoke up, it was often short of the mark. "Don't sleep with the girls until you get married, but you can masturbate all you want" was the standard line.

In an auditorium of 400 high school males, the students got wind that our assembly topic was about marriage and sex so they came in chanting "Sex can wait. Masturbate."

It was not the boyish bravado that made me sad. It was knowing in my gut, and the proof of statistics, that unless something radical happened to intervene in their beliefs, some, or most of those young men would be compulsively masturbating far beyond their wedding nights.

On a different day, at a different school, a coach bellowed across the classroom to over 100 young men.

"Take care of your own business."

I quickly learned it is tricky to be a female and tell a male he is wrong in this area, especially when discussing a hormone-crazed teenage boy. But that coach was wrong.

When I tried to downplay his philosophy and talk about the hope of marriage, his rebuttal was "You don't know my old lady! Boys you better take care of your own business." That summed it up for me. Out of the overflow of his heart, he was trying to teach the next generation of men.

We often condone in others what we excuse in our own lives.

Looking back now over a decade of teaching young men, as well as their male teachers, we can almost spot those men who were sexually addicted just by their skepticism, criticism, and flat out hostility.

They often approached male sexual activity of any form as a rite of passage. Sowing their oats. Working off energy. Harmless fun. Being a man.

They usually changed their tune when we asked if it is harmless fun if the sex involved one of their daughters?

But now, after ten years of the rampant spread of pornography, we push our message further — is it harmless fun if your son cannot be in a healthy relationship with his wife because of the self-sex he began in adolescence?

Rarely does any male coach, teacher, or youth pastor contest this probability.

Over the years, many respected Christian leaders have down played the self-sex issue while beating the fidelity drum quite loudly. Fortunately, groups like Weiss and Promise Keepers and others began calling the facts as facts.

Instead of turning a blind eye, they began calling men to wholeness, true masculine strength … and freedom.

Girl Talk

When my husband's pornography use surfaced, I consoled myself. "At least my husband has never been with another real woman," I sighed.

Yet before the sigh had escaped my lips, another reality sharply took its place. No, I realized in dismay. No, not a real woman. He had been with hundreds of *fake* women instead.

I remember calling a pastor who was a close family friend at the time. I was frantic and completely bewildered.

"What is wrong with Chuck?" I pleaded. "It is like he is sick or something, like he can't control himself."

"Maybe he can't," said the far away voice.

"What do you mean he can't? Just tell him to stop!" I pleaded frantically.

"Maybe he can't stop Jana," he said with a calmness that sent chills down my spine.

My heart stopped. Where does a woman go from here?

Clueless. Clue-less. One disturbing dynamic of this plague is the reaction of women. As a group, we are clueless. I was clueless.

I shared with a friend of mine the struggle and journey Chuck and I had been on and she admitted to me that she had found a token from a porn store in her husband's clothes.

I told her I was so sorry and asked how she was doing. She looked at me blankly. "Oh, I don't think it is anything to worry about. He probably just went there once," she said.

Taken aback, I tenderly pursued. "Why do you think that?"

"Because I think I would know."

"Did you know that he went the first time?"

"No, but that doesn't mean he is, you know, like doing it all the time or something. That's not his style."

Or is it? I think either from wounded hearts, denial, or just plain foolishness, women have bought a bill of goods. They either believe and teach their daughters that men just do what men do and leave them alone, or they have no idea what men are doing.

Our failure as women to wage war on behalf of men, and our daughters and sons, does a great disservice to the health of our families.

One illustration of our blindness is a women's magazine that I used as a teaching tool. It featured Pamela Anderson on the cover. Show that face to men and boys of various ages, they all smile knowingly. Her face and form is quite familiar to them from *Playboy*.

However, when I showed the magazine cover to these young women they know her only as a celebrity, as an actress. She is one more Hollywood icon to be modeled and applauded.

So I began to talk about pornography. As expected, their responses were of disgust and confusion.

I explain how Pamela Anderson got her start as a porn model, how men use her beauty to masturbate.

"Can you explain to me why we hail her as a celebrity?" I ask.

Of course you and I agree that she has worth in the eyes of God. But my point is that if you talk *plainly* to a group of young women, their *natural* instincts tell them that pornography cuts against their very being as women.

They don't know why. But they know that it damages marriages, and they shake their heads, hurt and confused.

One girl said emphatically, "My husband will never do that." She was countered with, "How will you ever know?" Silence fell on the room.

"Well, who cares anyway? It's just pictures right?" said another girl from the back.

Wrong. It's not just pictures.

24 — what's in a look?

God made our bodies male and female with great
precision. Nothing is wasted nor is it by chance. The
original intent of the Designer, remember?

So to minimize the visual nature of men is to miss out
on an important piece of the puzzle.

Today there are several resources and books that offer
additional information on the male emotional make-up. I
have listed one of these in Appendix A since they delve far
deeper than the scope of this book.

But to understand this topic, we need to know, at least
briefly, a man's biological reactions if we are to have
healthy relationships with men at all.

Doug Weiss relates a story about a man who owned
hundreds of cowboy boots. Why? Because when he
began masturbating as an adolescent, he was behind the
barn looking down at his boots. And now years later, a
severe addict, he is obsessed with cowboy boots. Sound
ludicrous? Only if you dismiss it as a man thing.

If you view it as a God thing, you see the potential
strength of man's design and the fang marks of his enemy.
A man's neurological system works like this: he sees
something he desires. What he sees registers through his
eyes and sends signals to his brain. The signal then travels
down his spine, which alerts his sex organs of pleasure
and delight. When this pleasure and delight produces
arousal and leads to ejaculation, the chemicals released

his brain are so strong they cause his mind to freeze-frame what he is looking at upon climax. This image is burned into his mind.

Within God's design, if a man is looking at his wife, into her eyes at the moment of climax, this is a very good thing. It creates an intimacy of great strength and bonding.

However, if he is looking at something else, the connection goes awry.

For the sex addict, what he sees that's stimulating, his mind burns. What his mind burns, it stores. What his mind stores, it fantasizes about. When a sex addict fantasizes he ritualizes. When he ritualizes, he masturbates. After he is finished he is overcome with guilt and shame. This is a chemical chain reaction that goes far beyond pictures. It is chemical addiction.

Why do you think Job said he had made a covenant with his eyes to behold no evil thing? (Job 31:1)

What got David in a world of trouble? A look from his balcony. (2 Samuel 11:2)

What we as women like to dismiss as boys looking at dirty pictures is actually psychological and emotional dysfunction that ruins men, families and careers.
One of the hardest things for us to understand is that pornography is an addictive substance, just like drugs or alcohol.

Here is a brief synopsis of the facts of sexual addiction.

First, it is a real addiction. Just like alcohol, just like drugs. It affects the whole person and has psychological, emotional, spiritual, financial, and relational fallout.

What is sexual addiction? It is the use of sex or sexual fantasies to medicate one's feelings and/or cope with the stresses of life. It may be a regular on-going behavior, or occur in binge cycles, but it is compulsive behavior that cannot be stopped without external intervention.

It is not a matter of will power. Hiding, lying or denying either the behavior, dependence, or severity often plays a large part in the relational dysfunction.

The difference between sexual addiction and merely

a "high sex drive" is the emotional attachment to the behavior. Someone with a high sex drive isn't desiring sex in order to fix something internal, and doesn't take a "no" as a personal malicious rejection. They don't act out with anger at being denied sex.

It is worth noting that this distinction does *not* diminish the fact that some men with "high sex drives" use their wives' bodies for release and not intimacy much like addicted men use pornographic material.

In advanced cases, sex addicts often prefer their world of fantasy and self-sex to sex with their partner. The clinical term for this is sexual anorexia.

Sexual addiction is not limited to men only. Women can also become addicted.

But there is treatment available. There is hope. There is a God who still heals.

Battle Cry

There is a war going on. Remember the Beast? The enemy will take our greatest gift, being made in the image of God, and do all he can to distort and destroy it. The attack on his strength and her beauty is no accident. We must stand. Our hearts are on the front line and they are taking a beating. Yes, there is victory but it won't come without a fight.

Before we can do battle though, we have to be armed, with truth, with courage, with Jesus.

I have walked through this hell myself.

I have walked with older women, whose husbands are in massive emotional trauma from years of acting out. They are both worn out from the battle.

I am also walking with young brides who are dumbfounded by the dysfunction in their marriage bed.

Their question is always, always, always "what's wrong with me?" And my reply is always, always, always not one blessed thing.

We must come back to the Father who calls us. The one who calls you is faithful, *he will do it.* (I Thessalonians 5:24)

25 — A faulty foundation

My husband and I were both "lost as a goose in a snowstorm" when we got married. I never understood that phrase until I got un-lost. Then I saw how completely beyond hope that is. Although we were very spiritual (we prayed, read our Bible, even had communion at our wedding), we were without a relationship with God. Think white goose in white snow. Lost and hopeless.

In a supreme act of mercy, the Lord Jesus rescued my husband first and then came after me six months later. We had been married less than a year. It is a great story of redemption.

At salvation, we were at least aware of our serious need to clean up. I will never forget the first few times we showed up at a very conservative church which later became our home. My stiletto heels and skimpy dresses plus other non-Christian tell-tale signs like choices of music, language, and attitudes were dead give-aways that we were new to the church world. I bless them for receiving us even if they were shocked and somewhat perplexed as to why we were there and what to do with us.

We were a bit of an anomaly. I had grown up in dead churches, in several different denominations actually. My husband had grown up Catholic. We had gone from calloused church-rejecters to passionate Christ-believers. We had moved beyond the rituals of "I can work myself up to God" and had been swept off our feet by God.

We now called ourselves the afore-dreaded label,
Christians. We were the kind of Christians that were so on
fire for Jesus, that if you came within a yard of us, we were
telling you about the peace and joy we had found for the
first time in our lives.

It was true, in a supernatural way.

The healing began.

As part of our new believer rigors, we began reading
the great Christian classics, among them C.S. Lewis's
Chronicles of Narnia. We found our lives being played out
in the pages of this tale. In the *Lion, the Witch and the
Wardrobe*, Narnia is a kingdom held captive by the White
Witch. Under her reign, the land of Narnia was covered in
ice and snow and her prisoners were turned to stone by
the touch of her wand.

Aslan the mighty lion and Lord of Narnia, comes back to
claim his kingdom with the help of the sons of Adam and
daughters of Eve.

When the war is over, Aslan goes to her palace and
"breathes" on her stone prisoners, bringing them back to
life.

It is a powerful and anointed collection of writings that
the Lord used mightily as He began to "breathe" on us.
Our chains of bondage began to break loose.

The abortion, prior sexual relationships, my brief
marriage earlier, and my distorted definition of a woman
— all these things were now under the blood and I was
becoming whole. I was thawing out from a long winter
freeze. Jesus was breathing on me.

My husband's issues were very different but just as
damaging — abandoned by his father, a family history of
alcohol and drug abuse, his own drug abuse, rage and fear
issues. The Lord began breathing on Chuck as well.

Any of these issues *alone* were enough to strain a
marriage that was already hanging by a thread. (We had
separated before we made it to our first anniversary and
reconciled.) To not only have them, all but also to process
them *simultaneously* verged on the miraculous. We laughed
and called ourselves a "high maintenance couple."

If you had asked me about porn in these early years of our marriage, I would have said — no way. Yes, my husband was offered a box of "stash" as a parting gift to take with him once when we moved. Yes, my husband had this odd habit of "going away" when we had sex. But he had *me* now. Based on my premise of pornography, (in absence of females, substitute with imitations) what did he need that stuff for?

It never occurred to me to ask him.

I heard his brokenness before the Lord when we prayed together. I saw the change in both our attitudes. We were growing. We had come so far in resolving our past and walking with the Lord. Our marriage was faring better. We were serving in church and were even assistants in a young married class and occasionally taught.

As I said before, God had opened up a door for me right after salvation to share my story. Here I was, the most unlikely of people promoting abstinence until marriage to thousands of students each year. There was lots of progress.

We bought our first house and life seemed fairly stable. For the moment.

Holy Heads-Up

My first dream came early in our marriage and shortly after we bought our first house. We had been married about three years and had been believers for about two.

In the dream I was watching a movie of Chuck and me walking down a road together. We were laughing and cutting up but then he stopped and told me something. I began to weep and wail.

I could not hear what he said in the movie, but I could tell that he was saying over and over again that he was sorry. In the dream, I was doubled over in pain.

I began hollering and calling out, "Lord, Help me! Help! Help me! This hurts so bad."

Suddenly in my dream, I realized the Lord was there too. He was trying to comfort me. I told the Lord "I can't take anymore, please help me, I can't breathe for the pain."

The dream then looked like a movie in fast forward. You could still see Chuck and me, but the action was moving so fast I couldn't tell what was happening. When it slowed down to normal speed, Chuck and I were way down the road from where we began. And Jesus was still with us.

I turned to him and asked, "Lord, what happened back there? What did you save me from?"

"Nothing," he said tenderly. "You will walk this road. It will be painful. You just don't have to see it all now."

But Lord, I pressed him, nearly frantic, "It hurt so bad, how will I ever survive?"

He stood close to me and quietly answered, "I have just shown you where you are going. You won't stay there. You will just pass through. I will be with you the whole time."

When I woke up I was sitting up in the bed, my face wet with tears. But I had an amazing sense of comfort. I had no idea what that dream meant except that there were dark clouds on the horizon.

The next warning came about a year after the first dream. I read this passage from Luke: 22:31-32:

> *"Simon, Simon, Satan has asked to sift you as*
> *wheat. But I have prayed for you, Simon, that*
> *your faith may not fail. And when you have*
> *turned back, strengthen your brothers."*

For a reason known only to God, there was a burning in my heart to pray for Chuck. I inserted his name:

Chuck, Chuck, Satan has asked to sift you like wheat.

But I have prayed for you, Chuck, that your faith may not fail.

And when you have turned back, go back and strengthen your brothers.

I was such a young Christian I had no knowledge of what the Lord had done for *both* of us. Awkwardly, I told Chuck about this crazy thing that happened during my prayer time and he laughed nervously.

Thanks for praying, he said absently. Wonder what that means?

Life went bumping along, as much as it could with our multiple issues. But God was very much on the move.

One day at work, I randomly came across the radio broadcast of a Promise Keepers conference. I had never in my life heard men calling other men to such a godly standard.

Wow, I thought. Christian men really must be *different* from all the other men I'd known. When Promise Keepers speakers called their attendees to love God and to love their wives I got so fired up. I prayed and interceded for the thousands of unknown men at the conference as I listened to them sing on the radio.

I heard the PK call to purity — the challenge was to be pure all the way: eyes, body, heart. No apologies. "Be a one-woman-man," they proclaimed. Wow I mused again. I'd like a man like that and prayed anew for my husband. But the journey was far from over *for both of us*.

With great enthusiasm, I encouraged my husband to attend a PK conference. He had also heard and was interested in the men's movement that was rapidly gaining momentum. The Lord is so faithful. The following summer Chuck attended a conference with a group of men from our church.

When Chuck got back home we began to talk through the conference topics. A benign conversation began about the PK call to faithfulness. When I questioned him about whether Christian men can be faithful, he became very uncomfortable. My radar went up. When I asked him if he was faithful, I knew I had hit a hornet's nest by his angry and defensive reaction.

Over the course of weeks, the truth came out that he had "looked at pornography" on and off since our marriage began, three years earlier.

But we didn't really know what to do.

I had seen the progress of his heart being changed and my heart being changed. Now what?

How do you handle bad stuff when you are Christians, we wondered, since Christians weren't supposed to do bad stuff? Our understanding on the God journey so far was that Jesus saved you from all your past sins. But what about present sins?

In church, people talked about sin all the time, but no one ever talked about *their* sin. We were thankfully too new to the game to know you weren't supposed to air your dirty laundry. So we went to our Sunday School leader for help.

He was a godly man. We loved him and he loved us and counseled us to the best of his ability. But honestly he was more uncomfortable then either me or Chuck.

He gave us a list of to-do's and to-don't's. We all prayed together. And he left.

Chuck and I talked openly about our life and our problems, or so I thought. We prayed again for healing and the subject was closed. Life got back to normal.

Or so I thought.

And as per the PK model, Chuck got in an accountability group. When they found out about what he called occasional porn indulgence, they followed the PK accountability group model and questioned him as well as they were able.

Everyone was trying to help each other walk in integrity and purity. But for Chuck, it was like he was the lone offender. No one else seemed to relate to his struggle. So he kept up the face of the PK man, but he also kept his porn. Only now he went underground.

The problem is, no one, including Chuck, knew how deep the Beast had cut into the Chuck's heart.

Still, we rode the PK wave. This men's movement was a God-breathed blessing. Neither one of us had ever had this kind of godly role model and it inspired not only us, but our church, our generation.

A year later, I prayed for the men in our church who drove all night just to be part of the Million Man March. The following summer I even volunteered to serve at a local PK event and bawled like a baby as the Spirit of God moved through the stadium of men.

I stood there spellbound by the sound of men singing to the Lord. It was then that I realized God was not just changing their hearts, but my heart. About men. And about me.

The concept of men who loved and were surrendered to Jesus was completely foreign to me. I just saw such hope and promise like never before in men. I got a glimpse of who they are and what God was doing through them.

For the first time in my life, I had real Christian friends who were men, brothers, that were not trying to sleep with me like every other guy "friend" I had known.

This whole season changed the way we viewed men. Chuck was for the first time aware he was openly cruising women and it was wrong to do that. I was for the first time aware of the need to honor men by honoring myself in my clothing.

Now when Chuck and I were out of sorts and my heart was dying for some attention, I didn't want to hurt my Christian brothers by acting or dressing seductively. It was the craziest of things.

As my view of men changed, my view of women changed. As my view of women changed, my view of *me* changed. God was taking out the trash and replacing it with truth.

And Chuck and I? We continued our dance. We laughed a lot and fought a lot. We helped each other in deep places of healing, working through the grief of my abortion and his father hunger. But we also wounded each other in deep places of rejection and fear.

We bought a different house. We did lots of interior

renovation with modern updates and bold colors. And we had lots of company. It was a fun house. It was at this house to our great joy and surprise that we found out I was pregnant for the first time in our marriage.

We were growing in our relationship with the Lord, serving in church, a baby on the way. Life seemed good.

The Second Holy Heads-Up

The second dream came five years after the first one. I was pregnant with our first little miracle baby. In my dream, I was overcome with fear. I began weeping in great heaving sobs. The next thing I knew I was sitting up in my bed just weeping uncontrollably. Chuck came running up stairs to our room when he heard me crying. He had been downstairs drinking a cup of coffee.

"What on earth is the matter?" he asked, trying to hold me. I kept pushing him away.

I just sat hunched over my swollen belly with my face in my hands. "Please don't leave me. I dreamed you were unfaithful. You left me for another woman. Please don't abandon me. Please." I begged him and wept.

"I won't," he said, "I won't, I promise I won't."

Six months later the war began. I wasn't armed, I wasn't ready. But the Lord was true to His word. Just like the first dream.

It was painful beyond words.

We didn't stay there.

Jesus was with me.

As I look back on over the journey, the Lord was after both of us. He wanted freedom for both of us. Our completely different sin issues were entangled into one horrendous mess. The good news was, we needed each other to get well. Funny how God does that.

26 — exposed

There was a terrible storm in the wee hours one morning. I woke up with a start only to find my bed empty of Chuck. I went in to look at our baby in the nursery; she was sleeping beautifully. Still no sign of Chuck. As I went downstairs I felt this terrible fear knotting in my stomach. I looked at the lightning outside the windows and opened the door to the basement. "Chuck?" I called and he came running around the corner his face white as a sheet.

"Are you okay? What are you doing?" I started to walk further into the basement but he barred my way.

The reality of what he was doing hit me and I felt a wave of nausea wash over me. No wonder there was such fear before I opened the door. Then rage flooded my heart.

"Oh yes, hell yes, I am going in," I said and pushed past him.

He ran ahead of me and gathered up pictures that had been laid out on the couch. It was smorgasbord of sorts.

For some sick reason, I wanted to see the pictures. I wanted to see the "other woman." Chuck was horrified. He wadded them up and put them in the wood stove.

I stood there seething with rage. My mind was trying to compute this scenario; I absolutely did not understand. I just could not fathom why a man would look at pictures like that. It simply did not make sense to me.

When I talk to other women, they don't understand either.

The emotions run high and run amok. There is rage at the betrayal. There is disgust at the baseness of the desire. There is despair in the face of such comparison. There is great, great sadness at being forsaken for a *picture*. There is sexual repulsion. And there is high octane anger. Gallons of it.

There was a contest, and you lost.

Then comes the desperate loneliness and isolation.

It is like walking through a mental mine field. Any word, memory or touch can trigger any or all of these emotions.

And just like grass grows on mine fields, there is this bizarre kind of love that keeps trying to cover up the trip wires. We so long to be his desire, his chosen one, that we as women will keep hoping to believe that our love is enough to make our man return.

But it takes more than love. It takes the Blood and the Spirit.

Fears and Battles

My hand still smarts when I recall the fight that followed that episode during the storm. I thought I broke my hand when I slammed it so hard on the kitchen counter.

"This is why you were so quiet when I blasted 'John' for cheating on 'Amber.' But he just slept with one woman. You have slept with— oh, my gosh—*hundreds*."

"How could you do this?" I yelled. "Now that I am so damn *vulnerable*. Now that I am a mother. You said you would never leave me. You said you would take care of me and our family. How can I ever trust you?"

This was not our first fight along these lines. Before the baby, I would waiver between pleading for and demanding change from him.

Before the baby, we would talk about "his stuff" in calmer moments. I would tell him that he didn't *need* it, and to just *quit*. Chuck would explain that he was *trying* to get better. We both were trying to shore up belief that it would be over soon, like kicking smoking, and life would be back to normal.

We both consumed books on men's issues. We inhaled Edwin Louis Cole's book on purity, *Maximized Manhood*. But we were looking for different things.

Chuck was looking for a way out, sort of. He was beginning to see this hobby was eating him alive, but he still really enjoyed it. I was looking for a sure thing. If I could just understand what was wrong, I could fix it, I was sure of it.

But all these issues heightened when a baby entered the picture.

I was enraged by his audacity to continue in this sin. I was devastated by his rejection. I was consumed with what I considered to be the competition. Which one was his favorite? Was she blonde, redhead or brunette?

And as a new mother, a brand new emotion emerged. I felt trapped. We had both wanted children so badly for so long. We had worked for a stable marriage so that we would have a healthy family. Chuck *wanted* to be a dad. The Lord had to bring me a long way for me to *want* to be a mother, but now I was one. All the more reason that I felt Chuck had ripped another hole in my heart by continuing this behavior. I didn't want to be a single mom. I didn't want to have a split home. He would have to choose, his sin or his family.

There was a whole new battery of ammunition poised against me. I drove *myself* crazy. What do I do with this baby weight? How will I ever compare?

What would it take to get back in shape, and even if I was in shape, would it make any difference? How will I protect my daughter from this blatant sin in our home? Will the Lord reject us all because of the sin in our camp? How will I ever love Chuck again? How many times can I go down this road and still hold on to my heart?

At this stage I really thought if I could just be someone, or something, *more* I could get him to stop. If I could be what he was looking for, then he would be better and

I wouldn't ache from feeling completely rejected and abandoned.

There were moments that I wished I was not a Christian. Because even though I loved the Lord, and even loved Chuck, I hated the responsibility of having to forgive him. I knew eventually I would have to.

"Forgive as you have been forgiven," I would hear in church. Yet although that verse was true it offered me no truth at the time. It offered no comfort. My heart hurt so badly, I could hardly breathe.

I tried to keep going, tried to go through the motions, at church, with our family. I was so lonely, so neglected and still I tried to keep the happy face.

I kept going back to Jesus. Do you care? I would say through my tears. Is there any hope for us? For me? For our baby?

In rare moments Chuck and I would pray together, and I would see a glimmer of hope. I would hear Chuck's honest heart pour out in prayer. He was running from the Lord. He was stuck in his mess. He was miserable. He would confess his feeble desire for change.

For a moment, my heart would soften in compassion as I heard his pain and I would pray for him. But the anger and rejection quickly returned.

I would cry over the pain of his struggle and hate him for his struggle all at the same time.

This season in our marriage was a roller coaster from hell. Even though we started going to a counselor, I would not know for several more years how deep this issue ran for Chuck or how long it would take for healing. In addition, I was still totally blind to my own issues.

The only confidence I had was that God was working. He was pursuing us both. Pursuing us hard. I was learning, however weakly, to hold on to Him and Him alone. The Lord had shown me the Scripture in Job, "I know you can do all things. No plan of yours can be thwarted." (42:2)

I was banking my whole life on this hope.

27 — trapped

It's hard to tell one story and expect all women, or men, to relate equally. However, I believe that we share much more common ground than we are comfortable admitting. Some women reading this are confident, some timid, some are truly innocent of this vice for men. Some of you are deliberately ignorant. Some women would never share this kind of detail, while some like me, long for a place to be real in their anguish, anger and bewilderment. What are we to do?

We made marriage vows, or we are going to make them. We have children, or want them, or want more. We have homes or want them. We have families we love, or long to have.

Just one small problem … men have a vital role in these scenarios.

I really suffered with feeling trapped. When I was single and unsaved, I could rid myself of leeches and louses. I could drop a guy who seemed to be "some kind of freak" and move on in my search for a "worthy" date or romantic prospect.

But I got married. And saved. Moving on to another guy wasn't an option for me now.

After spending years in self-help and what I call "relational throw-up classes" here I was in the thick of a dysfunctional, displeasing, disgusting relationship. And worse, I was a Christian and a new mom. I thought of those two factors — faith and motherhood — as the lock and key to my jail cell.

I was trapped.

In my opinion, few people in any of our churches talk about real things. As evidence to this statement, I'll tell you that I was well loved at the church I attended at that time, but our Sunday morning gatherings grossly missed the mark. Everyone would arrive at Sunday School class, have a snack, have some chit chat and someone would get up and ask for prayer requests.

More often than not, there was silence.

"Yes I just caught my husband with pornography *again* and I am mad as hell and hurt beyond belief," I screamed in my head.

But not a word would escape from my mouth. It just wasn't done. Not there. Not later. Not anywhere.

It is disturbing and tragic to look back on that class of evangelical, Bible-believing Christians. Our denial cost us dearly.

One-fourth of those marriages didn't make it. I think our marriage had survived so far only because we had already tasted the devastation of divorce. Chuck's parents' divorce wounded him deeply and my divorce after a brief marriage had contributed to the desperate need to make this one work.

But for our class maybe a dose of real truth and real life would have helped us all, instead of playing polished Christian games that everything was *fine*. As a group we had wordlessly agreed to look fine, whether we were fine or not.

I had a reputation to protect. So did my husband. Besides, we really did love each other. When we had good times, they were great. But when the darkness descended again, it was hard to breathe day-to-day.

I remember the day after the night of finding him out, I drove around in my car for three hours. I just cried and prayed and drove.

I didn't call anyone because who was there? Who wants to hear trash about one of their friends? Who wants to hear the same trash again and again, year after year?

Who can you trust to share this deep wound with?

Chuck and I would make a go of talking it through. He wanted instant forgiveness and let's move on. I wanted vengeance.

He wanted a clean slate. I needed to do something about this puddle of blood where I had been cut once again.

He really didn't want to let go of his coping method yet.

I really didn't want to be anywhere near him.

Who understands that? And worse, who understands the nature of this sin to be able to speak Jesus into it? What I got were spiritual platitudes. Pat me on the head with a few verses, vague prayers, and let's get back to business.

I was trapped, and trapped by the church as much as anything. I longed to be loved, I craved the strong-handed touch of a man who desired me. I fought hard against the temptation to *prove* my womanhood by whether or not I could *catch* another man's eye. I was trying to sort out the holy from unholy desires.

Can I be hurting this much, and still honor my Lord, my husband, and my own heart?

My Turn

That night in the basement took our battle to a whole new level. As a way of placating me, Chuck agreed to see a counselor. After a few sessions alone with Chuck, the counselor wanted to see me. At our first joint session, I was skeptical and bitter to the core. I knew he was lying to the counselor. I wanted to meet with the counselor alone. Everyone agreed. When just the two of us met, I told the counselor that Chuck was lying. "I know," he replied. "Let's talk about you."

"Fine," I snapped. "But this is Chuck's problem."

"He has his, you have yours," he said calmly.

To say I was outraged at the end of our session is an understatement. He challenged me, said that I was demanding. He asked me what it would look like to "love without controlling."

I protested. Do I not have a right to have a faithful husband?

Yes you do. Let's talk about why you are trying to fix Chuck.

I am not trying to fix Chuck. I just want a man who loves me, who will be faithful to me.

"Let's talk about how you control Chuck," he tried again.

On and on we went in circles. Always he came back to the fact that I was trying to *make* Chuck get better. I was trying to control his behavior. I was part of Chuck's problem. I would have to forgive him and let him go.

"How in the hell do I do that!?" I yelled. "He is killing me!"

He had me read from Matthew 18. Then he told me to read out loud the last three verses.

Matthew 18:33-35:
> *"Shouldn't you have had mercy on your fellow servant just as I had on you?" In anger his master turned him over to the jailers to be tortured, until he should pay back all he owed.*
> *"This is how my heavenly Father will treat each of you unless you forgive your brother from your heart."*

"What are you going to do with that Jana?"

I began to cry. I had no idea.

"Forgive him," he said plainly.

"How?"

He told me to make a list and go to the Lord. "Ask Him to lead you," he said.

I left and bawled my eyes out. Great, I thought, I am the victim here but it's my fault. How did that happen?

It took me three days to get the nerve to do my forgiveness homework. The list was long and ugly. And I knew to even open the door would be painful.

But I sat on my bed and got alone with the Lord. I read the whole chapter in Matthew again. The part about being forgiven much really shook me up. I couldn't escape the magnitude of how much the Lord had already forgiven me. So I asked Him to bring back to my mind all that I was holding against Chuck, every lie, every incident, every disappointment, every rejection. And then, I asked the Lord to give me the strength to forgive him.

I read through every item, line by line. I said it out loud, "Lord, in the name of Jesus, I forgive Chuck for '_____.'"

I would stay on that line until I felt released. I cried, I got mad all over again. I sat in desperation. But I finally made it through the whole list. It took a while, but I got through the whole thing. And when I was done, I felt *clean.*

I didn't know it at the time, but the Lord broke up a lot of fallow ground that day. Chuck was still in the thick of his addiction. I still had my own addiction to address, but this act of obedience cracked a stronghold in my life. I later realized, God didn't want to sharpen my survival skills, He wanted me to overcome, to be totally free.

The added benefit was that when the devil attacked me by reminding me of this offense or that sin, the Lord would bring up the list. I could turn the attack to praise.

"Lord, I have forgiven Chuck for that. I will not be tormented by this."

The attack would cease. The devil cannot stand in the presence of forgiveness.

It was another step toward healing. I survived the counseling. Chuck continued in his addiction. We kept walking down the road.

But what I really needed was some kind of outlet. I could not talk about this "elephant in the room" for fear of disgracing the man I still loved. I could not explain how my heart was breaking, and how Chuck was struggling. Everyone was so uncomfortable with this blatant sin that no one had any answers. No, wait. They had the usual pat answers. Read more Scripture. Memorize more verses. Serve more. Give him more sex. To-do lists that felt more like tiny Band-Aids® when we were hemorrhaging.

Crossed Wires

What I lacked more than anything was someone who understood that I wanted to be Chuck's Beauty. I needed to be *his* beauty. I needed someone to understand why it hurt that I was unable to flirt for his attention because he was pouring his attention on every passing woman except me. I thought I must have missed a pretty critical chapter in the Christian marriage manual.

In my Non-God manual a woman had to look *just so*, have sex *just so*, and work *just so* in order to keep her man. Because everybody knows that all men are prone to wander.

In my Non-God manual a woman lived motivated by fear and failure. Because if she didn't get it right, he was outta there. There were plenty of women willing to do it his way.

I erroneously thought if you were Christians those rules did not apply. I knew the PK mantra. It was supposed to be different. I thought if Christ was your "glue," that some of the world's talons just couldn't rip you apart. To my surprise, I was seeing the exact same relational destruction inside the church as out of the church.

I was still walking the tightrope of fear and failure. Only now as a Christian, I couldn't go openly flirt and dress seductively and recruit attention from other males to fill my attention cup, because now the "other guy" was my Christian brother. Now my sole source of affirmation was to be from my husband. But instead of my husband checking me out, he was totally checked out.

I kept asking, am I crazy? Am I the one who is wrong? I was beginning to think that as a Christian, I was wrong to desire this kind of love and adoration.

This belief was reinforced by two "truths" that kept surfacing in Christian discussions. The first "truth" was the thought that women should be satisfied by just serving their husbands and being good mothers. Their worth was in serving everyone and keeping everyone happy. The second "truth" was that men think about sex 24/7 and the competition is fierce so you better give up the sex to him, all the time, whether you want to or not.

I just couldn't buy it. There *had* to be more.

Wives and Lovers

Hey, little girl,
comb your hair, fix your make-up,
soon he will open the door,
Don't think because
there's a ring on your finger,
you needn't try any more.
For wives should always be lovers too,
Run to his arms the moment
he comes home to you.
I'm warning you,
Day after day, there are girls
at the office and
men will always be men
Don't send him out,
with your hair still in curlers,
you may not see him again.

- Jack Jones

28 — God are you kidding?

I think I learned early in my walk with God to be honest with Him. Not only did He already know my heart and thoughts, He could handle hearing it from me. If God was God, then He could take all the yuck I had to dish out.

What I discovered in my candid tirades to Him, was that I had two basic problems: I didn't trust God and I hated men.

I mean I had learned to "trust" God in the standard-issue God-areas — to save me, hear my prayers, even provide for me. I had already experienced His faithfulness in many ways and was slowly learning to hear His voice. But over the course of this journey, I came to see that I didn't really *know Him*, so trusting Him in these raw places was foreign to me.

Add to this recipe my wavering perception of men, and I had a mess. It didn't help that my hope of a PK marriage never materialized. I clearly did not have a one-woman man. On top of that, I was reading men's books which revealed the struggle for purity and I taught high school guys about saving sex for marriage. I saw the gamut of reactions, both in print and in person.

I was pretty current on the male realities. To put it bluntly, the opposite sex was less than inspiring.

So I really complained a lot to God about how gross men were, how shallow, how pathetic. How weak they were and so completely undone by their sex drive.

This opinion seemed reasonable based on my history of rejection. I had been sexually propositioned by bosses, teachers, professors, friends of boyfriends — I felt deep disdain pretty much across the board.

My hope in the Promise Keepers wave had flattened out. There was excitement about the "making of a godly man," but eventually the PK guidelines only served to set an impossible goal for me and my husband. Everywhere I looked, Christian or not, I saw the real life hurts of male desire gone awry.

I couldn't figure out where God was in the middle of all this mess.

So when the pornography bomb exploded in my life, it was like Hiroshima. It wasn't just my life, my man, our little world that was affected. It was real life. All around, all the time. The ash and acid covered many more miles. It poisoned, or revealed, the reality of being a man. And thus, just being a woman meant we were covered by the same ash and acid.

I tried to talk to men for counsel about what is a woman supposed to do? Some men, with utmost sincerity and the best of intentions, told me to look the other way. Get used to it. Get over it.

Get over it?

Are you kidding me? I had spent my whole life with a lot of stupid men who had told me to get over it. There just has to be hope. Somewhere, somehow. Now I have a new life with the King of Kings and the only thing you can tell me to do is get over it?

I don't think so.

29 — hiding out

It is ironic how our house purchases paralleled our journey. We moved way out in the country to a gentleman's estate with five acres and a house that had two separate living quarters. The land and house had been grossly neglected for years. But there was great potential. It would be a lot of work. And money.

We called it "Still Waters" because there were three large ponds on the grounds.

Of course we brought our dual issues with us when we moved in. But this time we actually unpacked the boxes. There had been several incidents over the years.

Lots of attempts at sin management.

Lots of "I'm sorrys."

Lots of "I'm over this."

Lots of anger, tears and prayers.

But the war raged on. I was on my way to a women's retreat when the Lord shut a very important door for me. I was churning because Chuck had gotten "busted" again. I never wanted to find out, the Lord just always managed to reveal truth.

As I was driving away, I remembered seeing the pain in his face through my own tears. Our little girl was standing next to him holding his hand. The picture of the two of them without me about killed me.

I vented for an hour as I drove.

About how I believed in marriage, but —
About how I have done all I can but —
About how I do trust God, but seriously — enough is
enough.
I wanted out.

All my words were silenced by His. "Do not ever speak
the word *divorce* to me again."
I began to cry. Is this my death sentence then, Lord? Is
this the punishment for all my past sexual sins? Is this all
there is for me, stuck in a hopeless marriage?
Only silence.
"Then change him Lord. Or change me," I begged.

Eventually He did both.

Jealous Wife

"How many times is a man going to get fired up by a
pair of boobs?" I asked ranting and raving.
I had called our previous counselor over Chuck's being
paralyzed by daring magazine covers.
"Every time. Jana. What's the question?" he asked
sounding bored.
"Look, I know that I am *just* a woman, but I am
unbelievably educated on the visual nature of a man. Give
me a break, to be stopped in mid-sentence over a magazine.
How long do guys do this?"
"Every time, Jana. Every time. Maybe you are just
jealous," he tossed out.
My head about popped off my shoulders!
Of course I am jealous, you idiot! I wanted to scream
over the phone. I have spent my whole life trying to find a
man that would love me, for me, and here I am married to
a man who doesn't even want me.
He kept defending men. I kept asking how that behavior
is supposed to be okay. He said, it's not okay, it's just how
it is. I felt like I was in a psycho-babble blender. Round
and round, we went. Somehow the conversation stopped

on my fluctuating weight and at that moment I knew my time with this counselor was over. I didn't know a lot, but I knew that Chuck's issue was not related to my weight.

"You know what," I said through clenched teeth, "no matter what size I have been, he has never been satisfied. I don't think this is a weight issue."

I went out on my porch after I got off the phone and just bawled my eyes out. "Lord, what is wrong with this picture? You made men so visually stimulated, but then You make women's bodies change a thousand times over her lifetime, and worse, we live in a generation where there is plenty of flesh to choose from. And somehow this monster always comes back to being my fault. Men are just so gross and stupid and pathetic. I hate this. What is the point?"

Men are made in my image, Jana, said the now-familiar still small voice.

"Well that scares me to death then. Is this what You are like?"

I knew it was audacious to wrestle with God over His design. But somebody somewhere was desperately off track. And so far, I was the only one who didn't seem to get it, or wouldn't swallow the line: it's just how men are.

Men are made in my image. I love men.

"Why did you make them like this then?"

Sin did that. They were made to reflect My glory. But guess what, I have not given up on them. Don't quit on me, Jana, because I haven't quit on them.

Warrior

A stronghold was broken that day. I realized that God was up to something. He didn't agree with the cultural acceptance of "boys will be boys" but more importantly He knew they couldn't get well by themselves. It was a war. And He is the great Warrior.

I picked up my sword that day. I could either quit and become yet another statistic or I could ask and expect my powerful God to show up. I decided I wasn't going to take this attack lying down. I stopped asking how to stop the pain for my sake and started asking what was my position in this brutal war.

We are all in this war already. It is just a question about what side we are fighting on. For the sake of any woman who might be reading this I want to offer the things I tried that *didn't* work over the last fifteen years. We get really muddled as women trying to protect our hearts, family, and world. I will tell you how healing did eventually come. But let me tell you what *did not* bring healing, so that perhaps you might bypass these attempts, should you ever find yourself in this place.

Here Comes Da Judge

Not every woman suffers from the "fix–it" disease that I did. But most of us have had a symptom or two. When I found out about the "problem" that Chuck had, I began the process of fixing him.

He was broken. No problem, I can fix it: armed with the Word of God, confident that this was a rare, *isolated* case of casual looking, well-read on the cures of the day by many great godly men, I assured myself that I would soon taste victory. (Notice I said, "I can" fix it, instead of "we can.")

I was determined to have a great marriage. I had failed in so many previous relationships that I would not fail at this one.

So early in the process, we were counseled to make up a

list of do's and don't's. It was called a "cleansing process."

Chuck and I had already given away our television years before. But now add to this, we were instructed no movies, no videos, no malls, etc. The idea was to stop all stimulation. Don't go where you might be tempted.

We all agreed that this was a good plan. Chuck told me he was sorry that this was happening. Chuck asked if I would help him. Of course, I said I would.

But several years down the road, we both found that our plan had backfired.

I became not an ally but a judge. A cruel judge.

Chuck did want my help and support and I did want to help him. But when he fell, it hurt me too. While he was on restriction, so was I.

The bottom line is, we were trying to clean the outside of the cup, instead of dealing with what was *inside* the cup. I had been assigned the designated judge to assess the guilt and the penalty. It gave me control I desperately *did not* need, and took from Chuck responsibility that he desperately *did need*.

It just about killed both of us.

The Gestapo

I really thought I was helping. We would go in the stores and see half-naked women on the magazine racks. We would be at a restaurant and scantily clad women would flash across the screen. We would be in the mall and the posters in stores would parade lots of toned, tanned flesh. So I would watch Chuck to see if he was looking, gawking, or drooling.

Then I would lash out when he did.

We went through all our receipts and bills together so I would know where he was when he bought gas. (Some gas station chains are known for carrying porn.) This was Chuck's idea by the way. He wanted the accountability, he said.

If I had to be out of town, one or two guy friends would call and see how he was doing, or what was he doing.

This created an atmosphere of constant pins and needles in our home. He would choose sin. We would fight. He would deny. I would accuse. He would defend. I would attack. He felt like a failure. I felt like a monster.

Over and over the cycle went.

He didn't need the gestapo. I didn't need the weight of being his moral police.

This may be a stretch to understand but there's a fine line here. There is a huge difference between protecting and participating in his recovery vs. looking for evidence that he was failing in recovery.

I can tell you story after story of how the evil one tried to set us up to get picked off. But there is a critical heart difference. During these failed attempts, my heart was to catch Chuck and expose him. He was so good at hiding his stash and activities but his outer actions gave him away. I knew he was up to no good and I wanted to prove it.

But this proof was not for Chuck's benefit. It was for my benefit. To catch him or see him fail brought wrath and condemnation from me. I felt unloved and worthless, so he might as well feel the same, I reasoned.

When the Lord began healing *me*, my heart became concerned for Chuck's healing for Chuck's sake. It was not an overnight process for either one of us. But it was a completely different way of fighting the battle.

The Fasting Method

I believe fasting to be a beautiful part of relating with God. I have seen the Lord use fasting as a healing balm, but it was not the miracle cure we expected. Chuck and I had been to church and heard a message on fasting. So we mutually agreed to try to fast on Friday afternoons. If there was some kind of revelation during that time we would call each other. But there was little revelation, and even less relief. Why? Because ultimately, we were both looking for the "answer" to his problem. If he could just fill in all the blanks, he would be able to kick this thing.

The point is, fasting was another check-list — a method, a gotta-do-that-to-get-this result. A formula.

The Sex Method

I tried approaching Chuck more. I tried approaching Chuck less. I would try to seduce him or I would ice him. But pornography is not about getting more or less sex. Regardless of what men say, or what some men's books say, it is a heart problem, not a frequency problem.

I know numerous women who try to "sex" the adultery problem out of their marriage. One friend said, if I can just fill his cup, he will be faithful.

I don't think so. It is a heart issue not a physical one.

Sadly the feast or famine technique was just another method, another attempt to find a magic bullet, cure-all, sure fix. It failed too.

They all failed.

Hope Deferred

I remember reading the Proverb— hope deferred makes the heart sick. (13:12) That's how I felt. Heartsick from believing that life with my husband would always be this way. There was no cure, no change on the horizon.

To be completely honest, I realized the depth of my heart-sickness the day I went to Home Depot.

The guy working there asked me if I needed help. I rattled off my list of stuff. He asked me what I was working on. Then he asked another question. Then another.

I found myself thinking, this guy is so cute. Boy it is so nice to have someone pay attention to me. I wish I had cleaned up a little better.

He asked me if I needed help getting my stuff out to the car. In a moment of insanity, I said, "Sure."

We were walking out talking about tiles and recessed

lighting but internally I was fighting, fighting, fighting. It had been a long time, but I still remembered the scent of seduction. Can I welcome this attention? Where will it go from here? Is he really interested in me?

Then with a KA-BAM! my thoughts zoomed way out and I got the big picture.

I looked at his inviting smile and my heart froze. The door slammed shut. Yeah sure, I thought, he is probably married, involved in porn, always on the hunt with every woman he sees in here.

Men. Ugh.

I got in the car and went home. There had to be a better way than a revenge affair. My answer came when I stopped looking for a formula to fix it all.

Turning Point

Some leaders would have us "submit" to the "needs" of our brothers and turn the other cheek in the name of mercy and grace. Some writers would have us pour all our energies into our love relationship with the Lord, since men can't measure up anyway.

But I believe God is up to something bigger. It reminds me of the story in Joshua 5, when Joshua looks up and sees a warrior angel. He asks him, whose side are you on? In essence, his answer was that: I didn't come to take sides. I came to take over ...

In Genesis, it says that God created them in His image, male and female he created them. We are united for a reason, a reflection of the Triune God who made us, died for us, and *lives in us*.

Yes there was a fall.

But there was also a resurrection. The resurrection which means that though we were cursed in Eden, we have victory through Calvary.

Yes that curse still has its affects. Her heart will be always grasping after him and he will turn from her.

But it is the resurrection part we miss. Real change

began to occur, over time, when The God of the Empty Grave showed up in our day-to-day lives.

What started the healing in our home was not more lists or rules, but more of Jesus.

30 — hitting bottom

Historically speaking, our marriage was an endless cycle of Chuck getting caught or exposed, me crying and threatening to leave, him begging me to stay, making some promise of doing better and finally the storm would pass.

I would calm down.

He continued in his addiction.

Some trigger would cause the whole cycle to repeat every couple of years, with minor infractions along the way. We had been married ten years.

Then there was the straw that broke the camel's back. We were living on the gentleman's farm. Chuck called me freaking out.

He was screaming on the phone that he had really screwed up and he was afraid he would be arrested.

Let me zoom out for a moment.

Hitting bottom with sexual addiction looks very ugly but is very diverse. It can look like being caught with a prostitute, passing a viral STD to an unsuspecting wife, losing your job when an employer discovers internet porn activity, being arrested for stealing porn materials, being charged with child molestation, on and on the list goes. This root of sin goes far deeper and progresses to greater depths than most men, and women, ever imagine.

As it turns out, his "bottom" was not on this list at all

but was equally devastating. For the sake of Chuck's honor the details of the incident are not as important as hitting bottom. In short, he had a rough encounter and his license plate had been recorded on videotape.

He was coming home, he had to talk to me.

"Don't bother," was my grace-less response.

The crack in the foundation of our relationship was beyond repair.

Despite years of accountability groups, prayer, fasting, Bible studies, temper tantrums, separations, threats of divorce, endless hours of analyzing the motives and rituals, attempts at forgiveness, this plague still gripped both our hearts but in different ways.

This was not a boyish stand-in for the lack of a woman. This was not a get-well-quick little temptation. This was not just about Chuck's sex drive. It was not even about my issues with rejection and men. Pornography had created its own battlefield in my heart and in our home.

My healing did finally come. And Chuck got better too.

The Operation(s)

I hate how God cuts open wounds before He puts a salve on them. But mercy sakes, when that infection pours out and is cleaned out, it feels so much better. Have you ever noticed the sting that comes from peroxide when it is poured on a wound? The clear liquid boils out all the germs and goo. Then comes the burn of the medicine.

When I was little, we were not so overly conscious about pain. What I mean is my mom and dad used Merthiolate®, you know the red stuff that stings like the Dickens. They would blow and blow but that crimson liquid would seep deep down and just burn like crazy.

Sometimes, medicine hurts. Sometimes, healing hurts. But healing hurt is not like the throbbing endless pain of the wound before it is cut open. With a wound, the pressure builds and becomes painful to even the slightest touch.

If left untreated the infection moves beyond the initial

wound and the sickness spreads. Fever develops from the toxins dumping into the body's systems. The whole body suffers from the pain.

But as soon as the wound is cut open, there is relief. Not healing, just relief. Then the medicine is applied. There is a process started. Still not healing, just a start of healing.

But healing is a good kind of hurt. Like a hurt of hope.

It may burn like crazy but there is a hurt of hope because at least something good as entered the wound site. There is hope of restoration.

This is how it was the day that Chuck called from his "incident." The wound had been cut open. The stench and pus and yuck just poured out. There was no healing yet.

Just relief.

But then Chuck did something he had never done before. He went to a man with a strong prayer and prophetic gifting. His name is John Dee. They spent six hours praying, confessing, proclaiming and blessing.

Think peroxide and Merthiolate.

Think boiling out the wound with the Spirit of God, then think pouring the blood of Christ over a hopeless, helpless deeply rooted wound. Resurrection power. It seeps deep down and burns, burns, burns. But it is a hurt of hope.

Chuck was not healed instantly. But Chuck did walk away from that meeting with a whole new picture of God. He got of glimpse of the smile on God's face, despite his sin issues. He got a chance to get all the infection out but then he had the gift of a blessing, a calling forth of his heart, a prayer of freedom, an invitation to love and be loved without to-do lists. *He got a taste of a Love that was more inviting than the addiction that bound him.*

We are now several years down the road from that significant day. Chuck and I both moved to a Bible study under John Dee. Really I should call it a God study. Because it was the revelation that God not only loves us but He *likes* us that made all the difference. We had spent years in the word of God and somehow missed that critical point. Chuck also joined a group of men who were working through similar sexual addiction issues.

Finally, he was with a group of men who were somewhere on the same path as he was. Instead of feeling like a freak show and thus pretending to be okay, Chuck was able to be honest with men who were wrestling with the same issues.

Truth was entering the scene.

The medicine was beginning to work.

Slowly, healing was coming.

We have compared notes on this season, and we see how the Lord individually molded our hearts to hold on to our hope in God ... not our hope in Chuck's recovery. We had both spent a lot of time measuring success by how Chuck was doing, how I was doing. Did he get hooked by some image, a double look at some passing babe? Did I blow a gasket when I saw him get hooked? Did he act out? Was he on the internet? Did I trust him? Could I trust him?

We were using the wrong yardstick.

Toppling My Idol

Using the wrong yardstick was a fatal flaw. It cost me a lot of wasted years. I kept thinking we were home free if Chuck was successful in recovery. But success was *both* of us growing to be more like *Jesus* in grace, character, hope and love.

We *both* needed a high dose prescription of Truth.

If Chuck's idol was a beautiful woman, then my idol was my rejected heart over not being *enough* as a woman.

I lived out of expecting to be hurt or bashed or rejected at any given moment. Now before you think I was socially inept, think again. I was very socially adjusted and outwardly "together." But the Lord looks at the heart remember? Inside, I was tormented.

Looking back, I really think that is why we moved out in the country. I needed to just lick my wounds and heal.

The Lord did several reconstructive surgeries on me over

those five years while I pulled weeds and planted flowers. I realized that just as I had seen that house and grounds as needing work but still full of potential, the Lord viewed me the same way.

The Lord was taking out all the roots of sin that held me captive. But He wasn't just pulling weeds. He was planting beauty.

Not just in Chuck, but in me.

He never seemed to flinch at how much care and work I needed because He saw the potential that He himself had placed in my heart.

Fear

The first surgery was *fear* removal. I had to face that I was afraid of Chuck acting out because of what that would mean to me, about me, for me.

Let me say that again.

Being consumed with fear over whether or not Chuck was being faithful or being drawn away by some babe, real or imagined, had to do with *me* looking out for *me*.

I have several friends whose husbands have been unfaithful either in the flesh or through porn. We have all had a common knee-jerk reaction to want a guarantee that it won't happen again. The question always pops up—what if he does it again?

Only there is no guarantee.

But God is still on His throne.

This revelation literally broke my need to be the police and the judge in my marriage. When I would have a flag about Chuck, I learned to say out loud, "Lord you alone know where my husband is, protect him according to *your* promise." I am not ignoring sin. But there is great freedom when you release other people's sin into the hands of God. Since He is the only righteous judge, it is a much safer place for me and you, and for the offending person.

Trust

My next surgery was *trust* implants. I had to learn to believe and trust that God was working for *my good*. Trust that God had put a *good heart* in my husband and inside me.

I had to learn to trust that God was able to keep the promises He had made. He could and would make our marriage altogether different. Not for my sake, but for His glory and His renown.

How did I learn that? By reading God's word, believing God's word, and holding God to His word.

Faith

The next procedure was *faith* grafts. He used *His* history of faithfulness and grafted faith into my unbelief. Faith is believing in things hoped for and the evidence of things not yet seen. (Hebrews 11:1 paraphrased) This entire process has taught me the beauty in suffering. And it has taught me how to bear up under when "for better and for worse" really becomes "for worse."

The Lord has grown faith in me even in the darkest night. And with faith has come hope. The Lord invited me to dare to dream again. What a gift.

The Lord was after my heart and Chuck's heart all the time. He could have used cancer, bankruptcy, you name it. But in our marriage He used our separate sin issues to refine the other.

Sound weird?

He used Chuck's wandering heart to point me to the true heart of Jesus. Perfect love casts out fear, remember?

Instead of clawing after Chuck, I could rest in the embrace of God.

He used my rejection and bitterness to point Chuck to the confidence and grace available in Christ. Instead of hiding or faking or manipulating to get his needs met, he could rest in the abundance of being fully known and fully loved by God.

Do you see how the man and woman are not to be fully satisfied in each other *alone*? It is through discovering full satisfaction *in Christ* we are able to pour *His* love into places that no human love can fill.

For the record, my counselor was on the right track. I hated the way he handled my hurt and my heart. But the Lord used some of his words to show me that I *was* trying to control Chuck.

But why would I be so freaked out about Chuck being faithful?

Because in every previous relationship, I had been *unfaithful*.

So now the shoe was on the other foot. I had chosen Chuck. I was and have been entirely faithful to him. But instead of having compassion for his weakness, I tried to prevent it from happening to me. I wanted to insure (read: control) the outcome, for my sake. I wanted my love relationship to be different this time. Which is a good goal.

There is just one small problem.

I could not *make* Chuck do anything — good or bad.

Only God could do that.

I wasted a lot of time and emotion trying to get Chuck to act and live a certain way. I spent a lot of energy building walls to protect myself from hurt, from a relationship that might cost me something. In the end it cost me everything, including my old ways of shutting down my heart and trying to control the outcome.

Only the Lord could do that in me, and in Chuck too. It's called *grace*.

Love without control. Love that is freely given, not because of what we do or don't do. Love only because Jesus died for us — His death and resurrection being the only way of evaluating anything or anyone. If He died for them then they were worthy of His love. Who am I to withhold what He did not?

We both came to realize that Jesus was taking us somewhere and He had every intention of getting us there. No matter what it took, we were going to be conformed to the image of Christ. The Lord just used our separate sin issues to get us there. Our hearts were being drawn to hope in God... not hope in recovery.

We were to *live the life*. Christ in us, the hope of glory. Let me explain.

Seeds of Hope

The Lord was very close to me in the darkest hours before breakthrough. There were too many years of wanting to pull my hair out for lack of knowing what to do. As the battle intensified, had it not been for the supernatural carrying of the Lord, I would never be where I am today.

There were lots of prayers, lots of tears, lots of Scripture. Through it all, the Lord started teaching me about endurance and perseverance. He used four things over the course of several years to give me strength to hold on to Him and to my man and my marriage.

As I share these four stories, may I ask you to step back a few paces for the larger picture of a God that is always working. These gifts of insight came to me in very black moments. It was not from an easy carefree prayer but from desperately banging on the doors of heaven. It was in utter brokenness and desperation that I begged the only One who could help, to help.

I am not offering a formula. I am trying to tell you that God speaks and He lives. For me. For you.

No more. No less.

31 — the promise

So many of the years blur together for me. Wanting to be whole. Praying for help. Wanting to strike out at Chuck. Praying for his freedom. Wanting to be loved. Wanting to love him no matter what. Just wanting …

And as I said before, the Lord was teaching both of us really that our journey was more about Jesus and His life in us, than about me or about Chuck.

That sounds really nice, but when you are walking blind in a pit of vipers, I learned that He really is our ever present help.

So when I got one of my divine 3 a.m. wake up calls, I asked the Lord what He had to say. As it turns out, He said quite a lot. He had all of Psalm 107 on His mind. Go ahead. Read it. Out loud. Slowly.

Give thanks to the Lord, for he is good;
his love endures forever.

Let the redeemed of the Lord say this—
those he redeemed from the hand of the foe,

those he gathered from the lands,
from east and west, from north and south.

Some wandered in desert wastelands,
finding no way to a city where they could settle.
They were hungry and thirsty,
and their lives ebbed away.

Then they cried out to the Lord in their trouble,
and he delivered them from their distress.

He led them by a straight way
to a city where they could settle.

Let them give thanks to the Lord for his unfailing love
and his wonderful deeds for men,

for he satisfies the thirsty
and fills the hungry with good things.

Some sat in darkness and the deepest gloom,
prisoners suffering in iron chains,

for they had rebelled against the words of God
and despised the counsel of the Most High.

So he subjected them to bitter labor;
they stumbled, and there was no one to help.

Then they cried to the Lord in their trouble,
and he saved them from their distress.

He brought them out of darkness and the deepest gloom
and broke away their chains.

Let them give thanks to the Lord for his unfailing love
and his wonderful deeds for men,

for he breaks down gates of bronze
and cuts through bars of iron.

Some became fools through their rebellious ways

and suffered affliction because of their iniquities.

They loathed all food
and drew near the gates of death.

Then they cried to the Lord in their trouble,
and he saved them from their distress.

He sent forth his word and healed them;
he rescued them from the grave.

Let them give thanks to the Lord for his unfailing love
and his wonderful deeds for men.

Let them sacrifice thank offerings
and tell of his works with songs of joy.

Others went out on the sea in ships;
they were merchants on the mighty waters.

They saw the works of the Lord,
his wonderful deeds in the deep.

For he spoke and stirred up a tempest
that lifted high the waves.

They mounted up to the heavens and went down to the
depths; in their peril their courage melted away.

They reeled and staggered like drunken men;
they were at their wits' end.

Then they cried out to the Lord in their trouble,
and he brought them out of their distress.

He stilled the storm to a whisper;
the waves of the sea were hushed.

They were glad when it grew calm,

and he guided them to their desired haven.

Let them give thanks to the Lord for his unfailing love
and his wonderful deeds for men.

Let them exalt him in the assembly of the people
and praise him in the council of the elders.

He turned rivers into a desert,
flowing springs into thirsty ground,

and fruitful land into a salt waste,
because of the wickedness of those who lived there.

He turned the desert into pools of water
and the parched ground into flowing springs;

there he brought the hungry to live,
and they founded a city where they could settle.

They sowed fields and planted vineyards
that yielded a fruitful harvest;

he blessed them, and their numbers greatly increased,
and he did not let their herds diminish.

Then their numbers decreased, and they were humbled
by oppression, calamity and sorrow;

he who pours contempt on nobles
made them wander in a trackless waste.

But he lifted the needy out of their affliction
and increased their families like flocks.

The upright see and rejoice,
but all the wicked shut their mouths.

Whoever is wise, let him heed these things

and consider the great love of the Lord.

Wow. That's all I could say. Wow. The italics are mine, because those are the buzz phrases that the Lord stirred in me. But He wasn't done yet.

I will deliver Chuck. Jana. In due time, deliverance will come.

I just sat there and pondered. When? How? Soon? I went back to bed and laid there thinking that this fact changes everything for me.

I could trust God more than I trusted Chuck. If God said it — it must be so. He could not lie. Who could stop God? Not even Chuck could stop God from healing Chuck.

It was like the Lord gave me a "shield of faith" in a brand new way. When the attacks came, and they did in great force, I would remind my heart that my God had said, *deliverance will come.* And I would hold up my shield and hang on for all it was worth.

And a funny thing happened. My prayers changed. A little more strength. A little less whining. A little more faith. A little less fear.

Confession

Part of recovery is coming clean. The nature of pornography is cloaked in deception. Therefore, at some point every guy has to face the reality of his choices and has to confess to the people that have been impacted by his sin. Hiding and lying are as much a part of the rush and ritual as the physical release. So as part of Chucks "group" session, their homework was to confess the lies and deceptions to the wounded wives. Chuck came home and laid out the last ten years and told the truth.

I thought I could handle it. I knew deliverance was coming. I was growing in Jesus just like He was.

But I was wrong. I didn't despise him or even feel

disgust. That season in my heart has passed. But what hit me between the eyes was the loss of the sacred memories that I had clung to. Now they were sullied. Tainted. Damaged goods. I listened and cried. I sat there silent and tormented as he just let the poison flush out of his system.

When it was over, he said, "Man, I feel so much better."

"That's great honey," I said feebly. But the next day, after he had gone to work, I fell apart.

All I could do was cry. All the lies. All the hurt. All the betrayal. What was left to love? Even the good memories had been ripped apart. I called a female counselor who comforted me that grieving was part of the process. She was really tender with my heart. But while we were on the phone, I knew I was talking to the wrong person.

I hung up and went out on my deck and actually wailed. I had my Bible on my lap and just wept. Lord, where do I go from here? How do I go on? He feels so much better but what about me? Does anybody care about me?

Faintly, from inside the house, I heard a voice say:

"I give you Zaph-enath-Paneah — 'the God who speaks and He lives!' "

It was my daughter's video, *Joseph*, playing. But it was more than that. Of all the movies she could have chosen, and of all the timing in the movies, here was an answer for my question. I was comforted, but still pleading, I need you Lord. I *need* the God who speaks and He lives.

I sat rocking with my eyes closed. Tears silently streamed down my face. And a picture came to my mind. Whether it was a vision, a waking dream, I don't know. But I saw Chuck standing before the throne of God. He held his hands out before the Lord. They were smiling at each other, both had such love on their faces.

And Jesus gave Chuck a white stone. The white stone from Revelation 2:17, He put in Chuck's hand.

At that moment, the Lord raised His eyes and looked not at Chuck but at me and asked me *"Jana, what name is written on this rock?"*

I said, you alone know Lord.
And the Lord pressed further.
Do you think it says lust, or pornography?
No, Lord, no.
Do you think my name for him is liar, or adulterer?
No, Lord, no. I felt my face flush red from my accusation.
Jana the name I give will be the name I had for him from the beginning of time. And it will reflect the glory of God. Just as he does.
Yes, Lord. Yes.

At that moment, the Lord gave me a taste for mercy.

For perhaps the first time on this whole journey, I had to confess my unwillingness to believe that *my sin* against *Chuck* was as great as Chuck's sin against me. It was different for sure. It hurt in different ways. But in the Lord's eyes, we were both in need of grace. We both desperately needed mercy.

And more importantly, we had both abundantly *received* it from the Lord.

It was as if the Lord was asking me how could I withhold from Chuck when He had so extravagantly poured out grace and mercy to me? If He did not view Chuck anything less than what was on the white stone, how could I dare question him?

Go mainly, mostly, majorly to Jesus, John Dee often says. To which I now heartily reply — Amen. So be it. The revelation given through the Holy Spirit was more powerful than any human conversation I could have had.

There were plenty of dark days yet to come. But the Lord was writing a history book for me. He was telling me who He was, who I was, who Chuck was. And *His* grace, not my effort, *His* grace, not Chuck's perfection, *His* grace would complete the work He had begun. (Philippians 1:6)

And to make sure I got it, several months later He gave me yet another kiss.

Who Calls You?

Test everything. Hold on to the good.
Avoid every kind of evil.
May God himself, the God of peace, sanctify you
through and through. May your whole spirit,
soul and body be kept blameless at the coming of
our Lord Jesus Christ.
The one who calls you is faithful and he will do
it. (I Thessalonians 5:21-24)

Just like years before in our very first house, God gave
me a Scripture to pray and claim over Chuck. But this time,
I was beginning to know what to do with it. The Lord was
teaching me warfare. He was giving me spiritual weapons
to do battle for my family's sake. The Lord was calling me
to hold on to the good in Chuck. The God in Chuck. So I
began to pray this prayer for Chuck:

May God himself, the God of peace, sanctify you Chuck
through and through. Chuck may your whole spirit, soul
and body be kept blameless at the coming of our Lord
Jesus Christ.
Chuck the one who calls you is faithful, He will do it.

I noticed that some of Chuck's prayer spilled over on me.
I was undergoing as much change as Chuck was. God was
calling me too. The God of peace was "sanctifying" me,
that is "making me holy," too. Funny how God works like
that.

Intercession

The fourth gift was the rallying cry of prayer warriors.
We have learned the healing power of banding together
with other believers.

Either out of shame or fear, or despair, or all of these

combined, most of this journey was walked alone. But at this point, Chuck and I were exhausted by the sheer weight of carrying our separate loads alone in silence. I couldn't bear what he was going through, he couldn't bear what I was going through. And it was just too painful to bring the magnitude of the problem out in the light of day. No one else seemed to be having any of our issues. So we thought we should just keep it to ourselves.

I do believe the Lord calls us to be careful with our wounds and who we share them with. I know He specifically protected me from women who would take a confidence and make it public knowledge to our detriment. But I now have learned that life is to be a shared event. The good, the bad, the ugly. We are all sheep. Sheep need to be in healthy flocks.

I have learned the power of prayer but more importantly, I have experienced the power of others' prayers.

The Lord gave me a handful of incredible women friends, who prayed over the years for me and for us. Out of respect, very few details were ever shared. But I knew and trusted that they were lifting our marriage up to the Father.

I have one dear friend who has interceded long into the dark nights when I could not lift my own head. I will be *eternally* thankful for Nan who looked past our sin and saw Jesus working in our lives. She never once flinched in shock or disgust or disappointment over either of us. Her deposit of hope kept me going on many weary days.

But what began to reduce the poison of this behemoth was *healing* prayer.

I had never even heard of healing prayer before this season of my life.

Relax, there were no snakes.

What there were, though, were seasons of prayer when our hearts were laid bare in the presence of the others and the Lord. Then together we asked the Spirit of God to convict our hearts of sin, to reveal truth, to bring forth healing.

Our small group was a powerful place of refuge. Our

leaders, Jim and Betsy aggressively came along side us and began to do warfare on our behalf. They were breaths of help and strength when we had none.

As I said before, John Dee prayed blessings of healing over us. He asked the Lord to do what it says in Romans, to "call things that are not as though they were." So John called faithfulness and trust and intimacy and wholeness, things that were not, he called them forth in our marriage as though they were.

And in due time, the Lord answered all our prayers.

I have learned invaluable lessons on the power of prayer, the benefit of transparent community, and the hope born of being dearly loved in the most unlovely of times.

32 — Root Work

I read the book *Waking the Dead* by John Eldridge. And odd things happened as I did. Like a series of questions about why do you — ? But the Lord kept bringing questions to mind that weren't on the page. He was showing me all the ways I cope with my stuff.

But then came the part about asking for your whole heart back and I whispered that feeble prayer. Lord I feel chopped to pieces. Please give me my whole heart. And that was that. But a conversation began.

Do you really want it back Jana?

Yes Lord.

It will take some work.

Yes Lord. But what else is there? What more do I have to confess, what do I have to do to be free?

Over days and weeks the Lord began showing me bitterness that I harbored towards Chuck. I was holding on to some idea of his rejection of me. I expected it and looked for it whether it was real or not. But it was also about my rejection of me. I had done a lot of great work up to now. However, this area was roped off in my heart with the yellow and black police tape: "Crime scene, do not enter."

So to this off limits place we went, the Lord and I. I began to journal about faulty beliefs. I searched the Word for God's definitions. I began to confess to Chuck how I was holding malice. I asked the Lord to cut out the cancer as it were. And just like the character He is, the Lord used an unusual prop to set me free.

As I said, at that time we lived on a five acre gentleman's farm. It was a fixer-upper and I had spent the last five years licking my wounds and hiding out on this farm. I was hurt by women in my old church. I was hurt because of the sickness in my marriage. I was hurt because I just could not figure out who I was in the woman, wife, mommy, world.

So I dug plants and pulled weeds and prayed. I shoveled pea gravel and planted gardens and prayed. I walked around the ponds and fed the fish and prayed.

On this property were two young maple trees that had been planted too close to the house. The roots were pushing up rock wall flower gardens that lined the sidewalk. When we moved in, the root from one tree had just lifted the rock garden wall. But over the course of time, it spread under the walkway, creating just a little rise.

One Saturday Chuck and I dug up the flower bed right next to the rise to see what we were dealing with. Sure enough, it was a root. It was about one inch thick and so long we couldn't find its end. We agreed we needed to cut it out. But it was going to take more time and effort than we had that day. So we covered it back up.

A couple of years passed. Every time I worked in the beds planting bulbs and mulching and pulling weeds, I would stand over that spot. The sidewalk was now cracked and bulging up. Our dogs would often go to that same spot and dig. All the way down to the root.

I would tell Chuck, we have got to do something with that root. Yes, yes we would both agree and never do it.

After a couple of times of pulling the dirt and mulch back over the root only to have the dogs re-dig it up, I just left it uncovered. It was so ugly to look at. I would get mad at Chuck every time I saw it. I could do most anything on the property with mowing and such, but I just did not have the strength to cut this thing out. And I hated my weakness. *If I could just take care of it myself — I would*, I'd say to Chuck in a frustrated fit.

But one day, a day that the Lord and I were talking about my heart being set free, I walked past this half dug hole and something caught my eye. I pulled back the leaves and sure enough there was the root partially uncovered but there was also some green color. A couple of random tulip and daffodil bulbs had escaped the dogs appetite. Small fragile green shoots pointed straight up in the sun.

There's that root again, Lord. I began my familiar complaint.

But there is new life coming, the Lord said.

Yeah, but it will freeze before it blooms. These bulbs are all messed up sprouting this time of year.

But they will be back in the spring. Look again.

I leaned down and looked at the bulbs. They had been too covered over by dirt, too deep down to ever bloom. But because I had let the root remain uncovered, and thus a hole in the ground, the bulbs had been able to stretch their shoots to the surface and the warmth of the sun.

"Okay Lord. I'll take new life. Even if it is right beside that big, ole, ugly root."

So I tell Chuck about the bulbs and the idea of new life. He was not impressed. But that Saturday I came outside to see him digging around the root.

My first thought was for the daffodils and tulips. Then I came to my senses. I asked Chuck if I could help him because it was a lot of work digging around this now very large root. He uncovered a six-inch section from the top to bottom of the root; it was now as big as a man's thigh.

Chuck and I stood and looked down on how big the root had gotten and how the bulging sidewalk crack had spread to the mortared wall going into the basement that was now cracking. We wondered had it traveled even to the foundation of the house?

Faced with the gravity of the situation, Chuck said it was time to take this out.

And so our dialogue began as to the how to remove it, how much to cut it, etc.

Honestly Chuck was more than perturbed and not really wanting to dig it out. He wanted the problem stopped but with little to no effort. Despite this, he began pulling the dirt away. And of course, it was bigger than we even imagined. Chuck said to me, I need help to pull this out.

He remarked casually, "I wish we had done this when it was only two inches wide instead of 12." I bit my tongue and only replied, "Yeah me too."

He asked me to go to the garage to get a pick and when I came back Chuck stood there beaming, head cocked to one side, his foot resting on top of the jerked out root.

"How about this?" he said as proud as he could get. "YOU ARE SO THE MAN!" I laughed. "How did you do it?"

"I just reached down there and pulled it out with my bare hands," he said. He pushed the root with his foot and it rolled over. I just looked at it, gnarled and ugly, mud covered and protruding. Exposed. I had the oddest feeling.

With a heave, he threw it on the pile we used for burning fires. And it lay there. Still very present. Very real. I would see it every time I drove out of the driveway.

And the conversation with God continued.

The root in you Jana, is like that root. You let it go, it grows. You cover it up, it grows. You disguise it, is grows. The damage is greater than you realize. You cannot do it alone. Chuck must participate. You must speak and dig out the root in your heart so he can pull out what has been placed there and just left to take over.

Two or three weeks passed. There were hard conversations. We kept digging but to no real avail. How to move beyond the betrayal and rejection. How to believe it could be different. For him. For me. And the root lay there on the burn pile.

On a whim Chuck was mowing the yard and came in and said "Let's have a bonfire. We will burn that pile out there."

Later that night when it was dark, as the fire danced in sparks and flames, Chuck threw the old root on the fire. In silence I watched it burn.

Chuck left for few minutes to go to the store. And I said out loud, "Lord how are you tonight?"

He said *It's a beautiful night.*

I said, "You got anything to tell me tonight?"

Your heart, He said. *That root is gone now. The root of rejection, the expecting to be hurt, the "never enough" lie, and the always wondering when and who would be next. It is right there in the fire.*

"But why Chuck, Lord, why did he have to do it?"

Because he has more strength than he knows. The two of you are connected.

"Cool. Lord."

I told Chuck when he got back. And we did a "cheers" as we watched the root turn black, then red, then white, to gray ashes.

But there was more. The next morning something was different. I couldn't put my finger on the leaping joy. I went outside and took a deep breath of new summer air. The wood pile was only a small heap of ashes. We went to church and during worship. I asked the Lord, "What is this? What has happened to me? Some thing is really different."

And in my deepest heart I heard Him, *This is what freedom feels like. The root is gone.*

I call these moments spiritual transactions. I don't know where I got that term. But it fits. Where the Lord takes something out and puts something in its place. Or I give the Lord something and He gives me something else, better, to replace what I gave Him. I can look back over my walk with God and see all kinds of spiritual transactions that are like these revelations written in stone, only they are written on my heart. And they don't wash away or wear down over time. They don't get written over. They don't fade or go out of fashion.

These spiritual transactions are like my skeleton, bones that God is connecting to help me stand in Him in a totally different way.

When the attack comes regarding Chuck, or an attack comes about my worth, the Lord reminds me …. *You are free. The root is burned up. Don't try to go back there.*

And the promise of the new life I saw in the flower bulbs? Less than a year later, we moved unexpectedly. And suddenly, instead of tending gardens, I was tending relationships. God brought to me young women who wanted more of Jesus. They thought I was so free, with so much joy. I still laugh and say, you didn't know me then.

Moving Forward

Burning up the root of rejection in my heart and the steps toward Chuck's deliverance were major God surgeries. Once we got over the initial recovery from our operations, there was the time of strengthening. You don't have surgery and go through post-op and then go run a marathon. We had experienced significant breakthroughs. But there was a time of just catching our spiritual breath. Trying to regroup and reconnect. We were letting the scars heal; they served as reminders of the war we had just been through. A year passed and we were moving forward. We were learning how to talk about our feelings, our frustrations. We were learning how to trust again. It felt like we were trying to rebuild the foundation of our home and still live in the middle of our home at the same time. There was lots rubble everywhere but we were making headway, rebuilding our relationship brick by brick.

But the war was not over. Perhaps you and I need to face the facts that pornography is and will be an on-going, never ending, always available, always tempting vice for every man we know.

That means our sons and the husbands of our daughters.

That means the men who lead churches.

The men who love God.

All men.

Yes, some men cope in different ways for different reasons. Yes, some men find victory and resist. But it is everywhere all the time.

Now we must add to this overwhelming reality, that

this plague has also produced generations of women who try to live out of the porn model of a beautiful woman — to be available for consumption in the way they dress, in the way they give their bodies, in the way they view themselves.

This is an emotional and psychological concoction that creates a Mt. Saint Helen's type of destruction. Think epidemic proportions.

And while volumes have been written to address men's stress and difficulty in living and fighting the good fight and how to overcome, not much has been written for women trying to cope with this Beast.

The pornography issue aside, my struggle with the Beast manifested in what I call the Beauty War. Yes, my husband loves me. Yes, I love my husband. Yes, the Lord is working healing in both our hearts. But I still have to walk through the aisles and end caps and see the advertisements that blatantly tell me I don't quite measure up.

That somehow my worth is based on my looks. That I am *worth loving* if I am *worth looking at.* Have we been so deceived by the Beast that we actually believe we are lovable only if we are beautiful according to some *human* standard?

The following story illustrates the tension that exists around the entire worth and worldly issue.

Chuck came home one day and said he ran into our mutual friend, 'Tina.' Tina had lost a lot of weight and everybody was going on about how great she looked. He was clearly excited for her and told me how he had bragged on Tina's hard work and perseverance. I agreed that it was great.

Chuck laughed about how another friend who was with him had said, "Yeah now Tina's husband (Jeff), can't keep his hands off her …"

I choked on the last line of his story.

My husband chattered on for a few minutes about other tidbits. I sat reeling.

"Hey where did you go?" he said.

I sat looking at him blankly. "Why only now is Jeff all over her?"

"What?" Chuck asked. Clearly he was on to other topics and was clueless.

"Does Jeff love Tina?"

"Yes."

"Is it Tina that he loves, whether she is plus 30 pounds or less 30 pounds?"

"What he meant to say is, isn't it great about how Tina *feels* —" Chuck scrambled.

"Don't change the subject. This isn't about Tina."

"Look you know Jeff loves his wife!" Chuck protested.

"Then why the new zeal and passion?" I challenged

"Every person has a right to personal preferences Jana."

"Yes but are they real preferences or are they cultural preferences? I dare say if we were in the middle ages, the wispy models would be considered sickly."

At this point you could tell Chuck was really sad that he had shared this story and probably even more sad that God had chosen his wife to dig into the Beauty War.

It's now two years later; our friend has gained some of her weight back. So is there the same zeal and passion from her husband? Has she ever learned to love herself?

Here is my point: I believe God calls us to health. Spiritually, emotionally, physically. But I don't think being physically fit produces spiritual and emotional health. For example, while Tina was in her fitness craze, her daughter bore the brunt of her obsession. She told her slender daughter that she was fat, and that she would pay her daughter $10 to lose weight. This is not health.

More

What is enough? Is more really more? Or as relates to weight, is less really better?

Does beauty equal love?

These are unsettling questions. But the simple answer is — beauty and love are only equal in that both are reflections of God. In His image. He is beautiful in every way. He is love in every way.

The problems come when we try to muster up beauty and love out of our flesh or desire or will. We try to become the source of beauty or love, instead of *reflecting* God's beauty and love. Even more dangerous, we try to evaluate beauty and love in others and ourselves.

Hmmm. Now who does that sound like?

Oh, I know. The one who wanted to be the most beautiful of all. He would not settle for just reflecting God's beauty and love. He wanted, rather he was *driven*, to be the source. His arrogance produced not love and beauty but separation and utter devastation.

Does this condition sound familiar to you?

You know and I know that we can nod in agreement on this basic perspective. But we still have to battle the More Beast. It still stalks my husband's heart. And my heart. And your heart.

The Beast stalks every woman. Whether we are loved by a man or not, whether we're thin or not, we live in the constant threat of being picked off by its fierce lies and claws. It hisses, "You don't matter, you'll never be enough."

So how do we believe the truth of God's desire for us and have that translate into our day-to-day living? The coming chapters will address at least a piece of that question.

We need to know how to fight this Beast. There is more than just our hearts at stake.

33 — white lies

"My sexual meanderings have nothing to do with my wife."

I have seen this sentiment all over the place, in secular magazines, in Christian men's magazines, in movies from the 1950s forward.

It maybe started out as a joke, of course. But there are a shocking number of men who embrace this thought. There is some kind of mental and emotional disconnect between their actions and their commitments to wife and family.

Tell that little ditty to your wife when she looks in the mirror every morning and knows that she is not the one who turns your head. Tell her that as a man you can really separate the two, your meanderings from your wife, and tell her that it really doesn't matter what you do.

And she'll tell you, that's hogwash.

When a man says that, I want to tell him to go read the second chapter of Malachi:

> *Another thing you do: You flood the Lord's altar with tears. You weep and wail because he no longer pays attention to your offerings or accepts them with pleasure from your hands. You ask, "Why?" It is because the Lord is acting as the witness between you and the wife of your youth, because you have broken faith with her, though*

*she is your partner, the wife of your marriage
covenant.
Has not the Lord made them one? In flesh and
spirit they are his. And why one? Because he
was seeking godly offspring. So guard yourself in
your spirit, and do not break faith with the wife
of your youth.
"I hate divorce," says the Lord God of Israel,
"and I hate a man's covering himself with vio-
lence as well as with his garment," says the Lord
Almighty.
So guard yourself in your spirit, and do not
break faith.*

It does have to do with the wives. It does matter. It
matters to male and female. Husbands and wives. Fathers
and daughters. It matters to men and their sons.

Here is a classic example of this faulty thinking that has
been passed down to the next generation.

Chuck and I were with two newlywed couples and a
single man. We were in the mountains all having a blast
playing in the water, relaxed and laughing.

The men were doing the classic show-off activities,
biggest splash off the high rock, most rock skips on the
water, you know, I'm the top dog kind of stuff. Man stuff.
And the new wives were doing so well, cheering and
hollering for their men.

Go honey.

You are the bomb Baby.

Give us all you got.

The young men, glowing in the praise from their wives,
took their fun and shenanigans to the next level. They
tested their strength with more daring, more risk. Even
as young wives, these women had learned that men have
fragile egos. If they had insulted their men's ability or
derided their men's strength, the women would have been
chided by the whole group. We would have thought them
unloving, *unwise*.

But later a group of folks meandered down the river
on tubes. Among the wet shirts and tennis shoes floated
down a tanned body in a black bikini. Instead of looking
at the babe in the tube, I just watched the five of them, this
next generation of tolerance. The Beast was on the prowl.
Everyone felt the tension.

The single man gawked openly. The young married
men were a little more discreet but still they managed the
quick, side-glance maneuver. They nodded to each other
with knowing grins much like little boys who have stolen a
piece of candy.

Chuck and I just looked at each other silently and waited
to see how this would play out. One of the young wives
sarcastically advised the single man not to kill himself
from looking so hard.

His reply stung. "I am not doing anything that every
man here isn't doing." The Beast drew blood.

In this critical moment of warfare, the Beast poised to
strike, and the married men blew it. The two of them just
laughed as if there was an unspoken understanding— heh,
heh, I'm a man, its my right to gawk, no excuse necessary.

"I can look if I want to," said one of them callously.

While they were punching each other in their mutual
maleness, they totally missed the wounding on their
wives' faces. The glow of the women's encouragement only
moments before faded in light of their husbands blatant
rejection.

One wife said to the other, "What do you do with that?"
The other wife rolled her eyes and spat, "They're *men*."

Now the women nodded in agreement and near disgust.

"But I figure," she sighed, "I know where he comes home
to at night … I guess I am satisfied with that."

And I wanted to scream, *DON'T BE satisfied with that!*
Women! Fight for your heart, and his heart!
Men! Defend your women from the Beast!
How is it that men believe a woman should protect his

frail male ego but then turn around and virtually slap his wife in the face with dishonor and disrespect? Where is the sense? How can that equal "being a man"? This selfish, harmful attitude does not reflect Jesus to a hurting wife.

In the same way that she has learned to be so careful of his heart and his ego, and his need to be "top dog," he must learn to be so careful of her heart and her need to be *his* beauty.

Those young men need to learn that in the heat of battle, when the competition is the stiffest, when the Beast would surely slay her, you come to her rescue. A *wise* man looks to his wife and says, you are the *bomb* honey. You've got what it takes, baby. I am all *yours*.

Who is teaching these truths?

34 — truth revealed

John Dee continued to speak real words of truth and blessing over Chuck and me. When I told him that I had familiar flags going off, he said, "Ask the Lord to reveal truth. And ask Him to tell you, even if Chuck won't."

Does that sound sneaky to you?

It was a breakthrough for me. And maybe it will be for you too.

Finally, I am beginning to see that God is working in us and through us and in spite of this plague in our marriage. He is drawing us closer. He is teaching both of us. He is changing both of us.

Women facing this Beast often feel beaten, overwhelmed, undone by the sheer size of the enemy. Yet the Lord is working still. And at some point, both man and woman, and not necessarily at the same time, will have to come to terms with a Living God.

Jack Deere, a Bible teacher and pastor, spoke to men directly about the choosing to walk with God. " 'He will keep in perfect peace, Him whose mind is stayed on thee.' (Isaiah 26:3) Men you can't think about Jesus and porn at the same time," he said.

If this wasn't hard enough to swallow, Deere pushed one step further. He called men to evaluate the strength of their will. He challenged the idea of helplessness and victim mentality. He called forth the strength of a man in his desire to walk pure. His gauntlet was, if you want it bad enough you will get it.

This is very counter to the current thoughts on addiction and sin management. But Deere's reason for this belief, though controversial, was compelling. He said to the men, "If you are strong enough to resist the will of God you are strong enough to resist the devil."

Deere acted out a mock conversation between man and God. Man was lamenting about how porn is everywhere and he was so weak that he couldn't help but think about sex all the time and he wanted to do right but just couldn't.

God's response was — baloney.

God then spelled out the facts, according to God. The devil is a created being. He is not all powerful, not all knowing, he is a defeated foe. God shut down the conversation of man's weak will. He said to the man "If you can resist me and I am omnipotent, then you can resist evil."

Maybe you need to re-read that out loud. Hear yourself say the truth. We are more than overcomers in Christ. Not by our effort and white-knuckling it.

But by His resurrection power.

I needed this perspective. Do you? This is where the truth of God is really important. Do we know who God is? Do we believe Him when He says something?

He said, we are more than overcomers in Christ. (Romans 8:37) He said we would know the truth and the truth would set us free. (John 8:32) He said, My peace I give to you, not as world gives. (John 14:27) He said I have come that they might have life to the full. (John 10:10)

The Beast is a defeated foe.

Is anybody else ready to start treating him like one?

In our world today there is very much a process to addiction management. But what I speak of is the outside intervention of the Living God, living in us, providing us a way of escape. (I Corinthians 10:13)

35 — no going back to Egypt

I would love to tell you that adultery and pornography is a tidy little issue that can be wrapped up rather quickly once exposed and "treated." However that would be a lie.

Rather, I remember wanting to throw up the first time I heard a counselor say that the normal recovery time for the addicted man is two years — from addiction recognition to sobriety. *Two years?* And then, she added, come the years needed to heal the damages to the marriage, that could be three to five more years.

I thought, I am barely breathing already. Two more years just for him to get to a place where we can work on us?

I'll never make it.

But I did.

God carried me the whole way.

I know people who have been on the journey to sexual wholeness for more than five years. That is not how long porn or adultery has existed in their marriage. It is how long they both have been truly seeking health.

I hate telling new wives that their husbands "can't just stop." But I love telling them that God is going to change them both on this journey. I especially love telling women that they *can* overcome the Beast, if they will let the Lord battle for their marriage.

I wish I could tell you that my battle with the Beast is completely over. It is not. But my spiritual muscles, and Chuck's spiritual muscles, are far stronger than they have ever been.

We have made unbelievable progress to which I give all praise and honor to Jesus Christ. He still heals today. I still cling to His promises of deliverance and His hope. But I want you to know the "rest of the story," at least the story to date.

There has been too much living to bring in all the details. But after our hitting bottom experience of five years ago, and our subsequent breakthroughs, the Lord gave us the sweetest of gifts — another baby girl.

Just knowing that I was again miraculously pregnant and that her conception had happened during the healing stages of intimacy with Chuck was a doublefold blessing. Here was something true and honest that we had created. Isn't God so funny? He brought new life out of our new life together.

The Lord gave us her name, Charis. It means favor, because the Lord told me the day I found out I was pregnant, that "this was the year of the Lord's favor." (Isaiah 61:2) It truly was a year of His favor.

A year and a half after Charis was born, the Lord moved us from the country place to a house that was what I laughingly called "back among the living." When we left the house and grounds, it was beautifully restored.

So was I.

I knew I had been released. I didn't need to hide out anymore. I didn't need to lick my wounds because they had been healed. He had restored my soul by the still waters. We knew that God had something brand new in store for me and for us as a couple.

Our new house is right in the thick of things. It feels sometimes like our house has a revolving door because of how many people the Lord has brought into our lives. I have said many times of the transition that I went from tending flowers to tending relationships. Instead of keeping people at arm's length for my safety, I have this unspeakable joy, an overflowing passion for others I have never had before. The operations on my soul by the Great Physician were obviously great successes.

How does that kind of change happen? It happens when the Spirit of God is invited into the middle of broken people and He stays there. Only He doesn't let us stay broken. He is always working out the plans of God. I heard it once said that God is not a pain-killer, He is a disease healer.

We are really, really different people now. There is more peace. More freedom. Our marriage is different, better, healing.

But the Beast lives on.

So when the next attack came, it hurt just as bad as before.

But I wasn't the same woman as before.

Same Old Song

The scene was familiar. The Lord woke me up out of a dead sleep and said, *Go find Chuck*. I said, no thanks. I knew what that meant and I was not interested. I laid back down to sleep. Ten minutes later the baby was screaming her head off which was totally out of the norm. I sat up with a start and again I heard, *I said, go find Chuck*.

The same familiar fear from years ago knotted in my stomach. I found him on his computer, the red glow of the screen outlining his face. He was mesmerized. By her.

The following days it was hard to breathe. The questions rang in my head. Is this another five years that's all been a lie? How many times can we do this and still stay together? How am I supposed to go through this again?

I went to the Lord and asked out loud. "How will I ever recover from this?"

When I opened my Bible, His answer was swift and sure.

Then your light will break out like the dawn,
And your recovery will speedily spring forth;
And your righteousness will go before you; The
glory of the LORD will be your rear guard.
Then you will call, and the LORD will answer;
You will cry, and He will say, 'Here I am.'"
(Isaiah 58:8-9, NASB)

Here I am.

He was with me. For God to answer and to use my own words back to me, was empowering to say the least. So in the coming days, I did the only thing I knew to do— go to the Lord.

I went back over and over to Him and He continued to speak. Give me strength. He did. Give me grace. He did. When I began doubting the whole journey and all that God had said and done already, He reminded me of truth.

Jana, you're not going back to Egypt.

God made His point crystal clear.

I re-read the Exodus story of the Israelites being led by the mighty hand of God out of slavery. At the first sign of trouble many of the people wanted to return to slavery in Egypt rather than go forward trusting God.

Yes, Lord. I am listening. I began speaking out His declaration to the few prayer warriors who were praying for me and for us. "I am not going back to Egypt," I said emphatically. "I will not surrender the ground that the Lord has given us so far. This is my land, our land. The Lord has given it to me and to us and to my family."

It reads nice on paper. But the turmoil in my gut and my heart was wrenching. Chuck and I tried to keep talking, confessing, praying.

Honestly, we were not making headway. Even when Chuck told me that he had just prayed the week before, "Lord do whatever it takes to make me walk pure in truth," we had little comfort.

The Lord had answered His prayer. But there was still

the mountain in front of us to be climbed. Again.

We were both tired. Tired of trying. Tired of fighting. Tired of hoping.

But we had made vows to the Lord. We had promised each other for better, for worse. We had two little girls who desperately needed us to stay together. We knew that divorce was not going to make everything all better. But what would make us better?

We had to decide who we would believe more — the promise and movement of God — or the attack of the Beast? Who would we let win our hearts?

Everywhere I looked, the Scripture spoke to me of warfare: of true fasting that broke the yokes of oppression, of divine power to break strongholds, of the Lord wrapping himself in vengeance to rescue His loved ones.

There was even one day when I cried to the Lord for judgment. "Lord will you not judge this case? Will you not decide who is guilty and punish accordingly? Will Chuck escape any penalty?"

And the Lord in a deep and frightening way asked me, *Jana do you really want my judgment on Chuck?*

Mercy triumphs over judgment. This verse rang in my spirit like a bell tolls once loud and long. The white stone flashed in my memory.

I fell to my knees. "No Lord, no. I do not desire judgment. Please show him mercy. The same mercy you have shown me. Mercy Lord. I cry mercy."

Now more than ever I knew that it was Jesus, the warrior, fighting for me and for my marriage. And just as the journey began with a dream, this part of our journey ended with a dream.

Chuck and I were in a cold war. We barely spoke. Out of anger but also out of just being stuck. What more was there to say? We were stuck. No amount of wishing would make us unstuck. The prayers had served to keep the hostility we both felt at bay. But we still didn't see a way out.

So the Lord showed us.

One night I had a dream but everything was just like in real life, our house, our bedroom, even my pillow. In my dream, I was terrified. I have never in my life been so aware of fear, I was paralyzed in my bed. My heart was racing and I was breathing so fast but I could not move.

When I looked out my window (which in waking is right next to my side of the bed) I knew why I was so afraid. There was something, or someone, outside my window. To this day I can see its every feature. It radiated evil.

I sucked in a sharp breath and pressed down in my bed for fear "it" would see me. The creature was checking the windows, trying to get in.

The dream immediately shifted to the next scene. Chuck and I and our daughter Salem were on our knees in the living room. We were taking the Lord's supper together. And through the windows, we could see the creature checking every door and window trying to get in. Salem looked up and saw it and gasped in fear. "Mommy what is that?" she asked in a shaking voice.

I looked at Chuck and asked, "Chuck what do you think that is?"

Chuck looked at me squarely and said, "You know what that is."

We finished taking the Lord's supper and prayed for the Blood of Christ to cover our home and our hearts, to protect us from evil. Try as it might, the creature could not enter our house.

The dream was over but we were far from finished with it.

When I woke up the next morning, Chuck was leaning on the very window the creature had tried to enter from the outside. I looked at Chuck and my whole heart was changed toward him. I patted the bed and asked him to come lay down with me.

His response, which was on track for where we had been for two weeks was a cold, "What the hell for?"

In a flash the dream came back to me. From start to finish. My heart was completely changed overnight. I knew that something had happened in the spiritual realm.

I looked at him and my heart was just flooded with emotion. Lord, I love this man, I thought. Fight for us, I pray.

But I held my peace.

Oddly enough when he got home from work later that day he moved to kiss me, which we had not done for days. And I kissed him back, really good.

He stepped back and asked me what had happened to us.

I told him about the dream. We sat on the couch dumbfounded.

A few days later, after receiving godly counsel about the dream, the three of us, Chuck, Salem and I, bowed on our knees and took the Lord's supper. We prayed a locking of the doors and windows against the evil that would enter in. We took back possession of our home and our hearts from the Beast.

It was our promised land. We weren't going anywhere.

And we remain confident that though there be giants in the promised land, our God will fight them for us.

Mended

You repair all that we have torn apart
And you unveil a new beginning in our hearts
And we stand grateful for all
that has been left behind
and all that goes before us

You've got all things suspended,
All things connected
Nothing was forgotten,
Cause your love is perfect
You are our healer, You know what's broken
we're not a mystery to you

We will dance as you restore the wasted years
and you will sing over all our coming fears
And we stand grateful for all
that has been left behind
and all that goes before us

And Lord you mend the breech,
you break every fetter
You give us your best
for what we thought was better
And you are to be praised.

Christy Nockels, Purest Place

36 — "happily ever after"

I know we have talked about my aversion to "happily ever after." But this phrase has become a milestone in our journey to healing.

Chuck and I made it through the following days and months. The Lord continued to speak deliverance and encouragement and He continued to lead us into deeper communication with Him and each other.

If you are tempted to ask how, it was totally by our choosing with our will to hold on. We had to choose to love, to forgive, to keep believing the Lord. We asked the Lord to change our hearts, and He did. It wasn't easy. It wasn't fun. But it was worth it.

In an almost comical way, He brought us to a place where we could look back with relief over all we had been through.

We went on a date and were browsing through a what-not store, when we saw a sign reading:

And they lived happily ever after.

We both stopped and looked at it and then each other. Then we busted out laughing. Loudly. People turned to look at us. But still we laughed. Then we laughed because we didn't know why the other person was laughing. So finally we stopped acting goofy and explained what was so funny.

I said, "I am laughing because I read that totally different now. I used to read it as if *happily ever after* meant: I will be blissfully, wonderfully, floating on clouds happy for ever and ever. Sigh.

But just now, I read it as: we are still happy *even after* all the hell we have been through. And that counts for a lot. A whole lot. We're still living. We're still happy."

Chuck took my hand and we walked out of the store, a quiet joy and thankfulness in our hearts.

You can imagine my delight when he bought me the same sign for Valentine's Day. It hangs over my mirror in our bedroom and is one of the first things I see when I wake up.

And they lived happily ever after … is God's story.

Part III
Looking for Glory

More than "more."

What comes into our mind
when we think about God
is the most important thing about us.

AW Tozer

Unhindered

beauty for ashes
a garment of praise for my heaviness
beauty for ashes
take this heart of stone and make it Yours, Yours

I delight myself in the Richest of Fare
trading all that I've had for all that is better
a garment of praise for my heaviness
You are the greatest taste
You're the richest of fare

by Shane Barnard and Kendall Combes

37 — heart of stone

*Then I will sprinkle clean water on you, and you
will be clean; I will cleanse you from all your
filthiness and from all your idols. Moreover, I
will give you a new heart and put a new spirit
within you; and I will remove the heart of stone
from your flesh and give you a heart of flesh. I
will put My Spirit within you and cause you to
walk in My statutes, and you will be careful to
observe My ordinances. You will live in the land
that I gave to your forefathers; so you will be My
people, and I will be your God.
(Ezekiel 36:25-28 NASB)*

Take this heart of stone and make it yours. It really was
that simple. And that hard. To take something as hard as a
stone, my heart, and turn it into a heart of flesh — beauty
for ashes, as it were.

Dwell on that a minute. Ashes. Burned beyond
recognition. Substance and form reduced to charred,
grey dust. Now think of something beautiful coming
out of an ash heap. Something wonderful, breath-taking,
confounding — out of a pile of ashes.

Who can do that?

God can.

*See, I am doing a new thing!
Now it springs up; do you not perceive it?*

*I am making a way in the desert
and streams in the wasteland. (Isaiah 43:19)*

Take this heart of stone and make it yours.

It's not that I really DID anything to change my heart of stone. But rather I became increasingly aware that HE was doing something. This powerful journey of heartache resulting in intimacy, the incredible story of redemption of my heart and my marriage, all this is what God was doing. His plans, His goals, His desires. And He has even more on the horizon for me, for us. For you.

Nothing thwarts the plans of God.

And what is His plan for us?

Beauty for ashes.

God uses many experiences, or tools, in life to persuade us to turn to Him. But often these "tools" look different from our expectations. We want blessing and favor. We want to be comfortable and safe. We want guarantees of success and privilege.

However. While it has been my experience that God is truly lavish in His blessings and expressions of love toward us, His tools of persuasion *do not* guarantee everything will go well, at least well according to our definition. There is just no way to force life to go easily and smoothly. I believe suffering is one of the greatest gifts in the kingdom of God. Just look at the cross. This God is not concerned about comfort zones. He is zealous for glory, for righteousness, for holiness, for His image to be seen in His creations. (Isaiah 9:6-7)

When we suffer we have to face our frailty and faults. Our failures. We have to finally come to grips with being small and helpless. But I am learning that failing does not mean losing faith.

In our weaknesses, the grace of God blazes and His glory shines the brightest. Why?

Because any measure of self-sufficiency, self-worth and self-esteem has been burned up. Ashes.

It leaves only His beauty to be adored.

This is a familiar story but one worth repeating.

Renowned artist, Michelangelo was said to have believed that an image already existed in each piece of marble he selected. But it needed to be freed from the stone. When asked how he created the masterpiece sculpture of David, his response was said to have been — "I just knocked everything off that didn't look like David."

The first time I heard that story I welled up in tears. Even now it moves me deeply in my spirit. It is a powerful picture of our God.

He is the original designer. We are His masterpieces.

He sees us as His sons and daughters of glory and we are trapped inside this hunk of marble called life. With great power and precision, He does whatever it takes to reveal *the you, the me*, that He sees deep inside the cold hard stone.

What we call suffering, heartache, wrenching loss, rejection and wounding — God calls a chisel and hammer.

What we call hard times, God calls release. With His mighty blows, chips and dust flying, with his tender tapping and holy sandpaper, He shows us His mind is set on our freedom, our release.

Release from all that hinders us from being what He has created us to be.

Christ in you the hope of glory. (Colossians 1:27)

For we are God's workmanship prepared in advance to do good works that we might walk in them. (Ephesians 2:10)

Release from all that keeps us from being *with Him*.

What we call broken and beyond repair — He calls beauty from ashes.

He carves and cuts and chisels until we are free. Take this heart of stone, and make it yours. He is unstoppable.

It is the hope of God's glory that fuels change. And this hope is based on the very great promises fulfilled in Christ. Christ is IN us. His glory IS IN us. Not by our doing but by *God's* doing. There is an unveiling happening here. There is a transformation underway.

There is an unleashing of glory on the horizon.

Unhindered.

I love that word. Unhindered. Sounds wild and unpredictable. It's like being on a boat in the middle of the ocean during a great gale. You think you are safe on the boat. You think you are in control. But the reality, the ever-present reality, is that you are floating on top of something much, much larger than your boat. You can feel the surge and pull of the water beneath you and the wind engulfing you. The power surrounding you is electric. In that moment you realize your own frailty, and that you are very, very small.

In this picture, Christ could be perceived as the ocean. And yet.

Christ has even more beauty, strength, depth, and fullness than the ocean. His glory is fathomless. Yet He allows us, wants us, helps us to join in the experience of His glory. When we recognize Him, we come to understand that our little boats and all their finery, rest on Him. He wants us to enjoy the ride certainly. But the Lord wants us to look to the source, or ocean, and not to ourselves, not to the boat. We see that He is all and in all. (Colossians 3:11)

Therefore we have this hope as an anchor for our souls... (Hebrew 6:13)

My hope is built on nothing less
Than Jesus' blood and righteousness.
I dare not trust the sweetest frame,
But wholly trust in Jesus' Name.

On Christ the solid Rock I stand,
All other ground is sinking sand;
All other ground is sinking sand.

When darkness seems to hide His face,
I rest on His unchanging grace.
In every high and stormy gale,
My anchor holds within the veil.

Solid Rock by Bradbury and Mote

Christ in you, the hope of Glory. My challenge is to take off the churchy glasses that use the lenses of "I am a wreck, a sinner, an enemy of God" and focus clearly instead on the wonderful face of Jesus. Just how good is the good news of Christ?

Paul said he was the chief of sinners, but sometimes I want to argue that point. I was an adulteress, a murderer, malicious, vile...Need I say more?

But through Christ, I am those things no more. Neither are you. All of God's wrath, meaning, all the rightful anger and thirst for vengeance, the boiling rage over my sin and your sin, God poured out on His son.

If I wallow in my sin, stuck and helpless, I mock the blood of Jesus. The same is true if I wink at my sin. If I give a flippant nod in the direction of the cross, like a man calling a waiter, I mock the blood of Jesus. You and I stand before God completely restored because of the great wrath, the justified anger He poured out on Jesus. Such a sacrifice leaves only His love to be poured out on me. On you. This humbles me to my knees.

And when I stand again, this time in Christ, I am no longer the enemy of God.

So who am I now and who are you? The Lord says we are beloved, crowned with glory and honor, sons and daughters of glory — His *delight*.

Are we so honored because of what we bring to table? Of course not. Because of who He is, I am. Because of who He is, you are.

So as we explore glory, we look to the Creator to be our source, our motivation, our hope. And above all things, we look to Jesus to be the only one to define us.

All other ground is sinking sand.

"Therefore I am now going to allure her;
I will lead her into the desert
and speak tenderly to her.
There I will give her back her vineyards,
and will make the Valley of Achor a door of
hope. .
There she will sing as in the days of her
youth, as in the day she came up out of Egypt.
In that day," declares the Lord,
you will call me 'my husband';
you will no longer call me 'my master.'"
                        (Hosea 2:14-16)

38 — Spirit of Truth

I am not a Bible scholar, but I am a Bible student. I seek the Lord and expect Him to teach me through His Word. He promised He would do this through His Spirit. In fact, the Bible says the Spirit will guide us into all truth. (John 16:13) It is a journey.

Obviously, it has been a long journey for me and I am still walking, still learning.

The journey is far from over. Yes, I am closer to the Lord than I was five years ago. But my prayer is that I will be closer to the Lord five years from now than I am today. I pray the same for you.

The point is, we must take the journey step by step. Day by day. I do want to share some of my notes along the way in hopes that it will help you. But the truth I have learned is same truth you must learn for your journey — go to Jesus. Like the hymn, Turn your Eyes says:

> Look full on his wonderful face.
> And the things of earth
> will grow strangely dim
> In the light of his glory and grace.

With our eyes set on glory, let's pause for a moment and look at the ground we've covered: The Bible says we are designed for glory. We are created to be beautiful because we are made in His image.

The Beast is a constant threat to our definition and he is ever seeking to destroy and devour. We ignore him to our own peril. God offers us a unique and intimate relationship that is built through the Word and worship. All this happens as we walk through the joys and heartaches of life.

That's quite a lot we've been through but it's not over yet. As promised, there is even more.

I had a haunting question about the *point* of male and female. I really wanted to know the purpose of a female. Was the purpose of a woman just to help the man? This is what I was taught, implicitly or explicitly. We are to have his kids, give him sex, clean his house, be his "helper." And if that was really the sum total of God's design then why did it feel like there was an untapped region in my heart? If God is for me, then why would God's design hurt so much?

Rebellion.

In the past, when I dared pose these questions I was told I was in rebellion. Maybe you have been told similar lies. Instead of answering the question about God's design or even the vacuum in my heart, I was told to be submissive to my husband. I can still hear the pastor's finger pounding on his Bible, "Well let me tell you" — thump, thump, thump — "right here in the beginning" — thump, thump, thump — "the woman rebelled in the garden" — thump, thump, thump. Then he would read:

"Your desire will be for your husband,
and he will rule over you." (Genesis 3:16)

'See, right here it is...' the story would go every time from different pastors, different churches. The common male response sounded something akin to — you hate it that he is to rule over you so you fight it. The problem is not your aching heart, the problem is that you're rebellious, plain and simple. Bible closed. Get back to the kitchen.

Okay then, I would think and walk away mumbling and still confused, still balking, still wondering how God could bail on half of His creation.

I walked around mumbling and straining in this definition of a woman for years. I tried to do womanhood their way, but it just didn't fit. I didn't fit. I was frustrated and often isolated. "What's wrong with me?" I would ask the Lord. If this is what I am supposed to be, then why is it so hard? Why does it seem impossible for me?

Frankly, a lot of the women around me seemed in a similar condition.

We live in a culture that puts women in their places… places like the nursery, the kitchen and behind every man in the church. Go figure.

Before you throw this book down, listen to my whole point.

I am the woman who went into Babies-R-Us and about passed out. After 45 minutes of wandering around lost in a daze, I asked the clerk for an item I called an "OH-na-see."

With a broad sweep of her hand she told me with a comic disdain that the item I was seeking was called a "ONE-sie." Excuse *me*.

And the kitchen? Well, I am Southern born and country bred. I love to cook. I think homemade cooking is good therapy for me, good for our families, and dare I say it, good for our marriages. I thoroughly enjoy cooking for guests and even use my skills to cater weddings and events. My husband brags on my special feminine touches around our home and in entertaining. He calls these giftings the "womanly arts." I love that. It *is* like an art form.

But you know, it's the craziest thing, "ONEsies" and cooking just didn't address the "more" longing in my heart.

I have even, through God's grace, come to love men. I can name many, many men I highly respect and love. About ten years ago, that was a very short list. However, despite this progress, I still don't think I am to be "under" every man in the church simply because of the differences in our anatomy. I still don't think God is one of those tragic parents who *favors* sons and *tolerates* daughters.

For me, trying to navigate this rigid system of men's and women's roles felt a lot like being a steel marble whirling around inside a pinball machine. I set off lights and bells everywhere I went.

"Why? Says who?" was my mantra as I was told over and over, *you can't do that.*

Once when I challenged these hands-off zones, I was told by one sweet Evangelical Christian woman that "perhaps you would be more comfortable at the church across the street." The major problem was that the church across the street was a Universal Unitarian church. Did that mean you couldn't be a woman and a Christian unless you did it their way?

As a new Christian I baffled most, and outraged a few when I did not take my husband's last name. It was really sad.

Of all the areas in my life that needed gentle instruction and healing, the spot that got picked at the most was the area that offended some of the church members' sense of submission. People who never talked to me, especially women, would ask why I hadn't taken my husband's name. They didn't ask how can I help you *walk with God*, but how can I help you *get in line*.

Little did they know this name thing was a protective measure. With my history, I couldn't go all the way with the merging of names because I was scared my marriage wouldn't make it.

It didn't seem safe to reveal this hurt in such a polished environment. So instead I threw out comments that went off like grenades. "I already have a name," or "I don't need a husband to get a name," I said. You can imagine the reactions.

But can you also imagine the balm to my *heart* when Dan Riley, the pastor who led Chuck to Christ and baptized both of us, gave me a new Bible engraved with my *maiden* name? Dan knew that God was working mightily in my life. He trusted God with the details. Dan was more concerned about the relationship than the rules.

Relax, I finally did take my husband's last name. But it wasn't from the pressure I received. It was because the Lord healed some areas in my heart about trust and oneness. My name change was motivated by God's heart rather than man's rules.

W_{omen} W_{alls}

The last name issue was just the beginning of my banging against the *woman walls*. As I began to grow in the Lord and He began to unveil His giftings in me, my fists beat harder on the invisible barriers, walls that connected to pre-formed boxes that we as women were to fit in and sit in, quietly.

Thankfully, God brought a man to serve on the same committee as I did; he sheltered me from the "you can't do that because you're a woman" syndrome. I am forever grateful to Gordon, who saw me as a woman, not an inferior. He allowed me to pursue and risk, succeed and fail in many projects that otherwise would have likely been off-limits.

But this kind of battle persisted for years on different fronts. If you haven't faced this personally, let me give you some examples. I had been asked by a pastor to help lead worship when a young deacon told me that I could not read Psalm 150 aloud to the congregation as part of that worship because I had no authority to speak. Out of reverence for Jesus, I complied. But after the service my husband confronted the deacon's reasoning. Chuck said, "She had my authority as her husband, the pastor's authority and the Lord's authority. How much more *authority* did she need?"

Chuck was totally my hero that day.

I was a guest speaker in another church and was told I could not stand at the pulpit to give my testimony. It was for men only.

There was a pastor interviewing for a new position. When I tried to tell search committee members that I had a strong warning about his lack of purity, I was dismissed as too forward. The pastor was hired and later resigned due to sexual misconduct.

I had concerns about a Christian school policy where my daughter was enrolled. Their particular bent on women's roles seemed unnecessarily emphasized at this non-denominational school. In short, they encouraged men as leaders and women as mommies. So I prayerfully wrote a letter to the *all male* board explaining that their "bent" was not the only biblical interpretation regarding women nor was it the primary function of the school. I never even received an answer.

I can't tell you how many times I have approached a male person about topics of mutual interests, only to have his response be directed back to my husband. Chuck would ask, "Why don't you talk to Jana about this?"

Hem and haw. Shuffle, mumble.

If I expressed any opinion that countered my husband's opinion, the rumors spread that "We know who wears the pants in that family."

If I heard one more teaching on a "quiet and gentle spirit" or the politically correct version of the Proverbs 31 woman, I just knew I was going to throw up.

All these years, my heart longed to be a called out of these boxes women had been shoved into. My prayers were to be set free. Not as the sidekick, or housekeeper, or escort service, but as an equal partner.

Not for power, but for something deeper.

I thought God was trying to tell me, tell us all, something about himself when He made us male and female in His image.

I wanted to know the original intent of the designer. What was God up to when He made the sexes?

How it is that the church never seemed to read Galations 3:28-29 which says:

> *There is neither Jew nor Greek, slave nor free,* **male nor female**, *for you are all* **one** *in Christ Jesus.*

If you belong to Christ, then you are Abra-
ham's seed, and heirs according to the promise.

Heirs? What promise? The cross reference of verse 29
takes you to Romans 8:

For you did not receive a spirit that makes
you a slave again to fear, but you received the
Spirit of sonship. And by him we cry, "Abba, Fa-
ther." The Spirit himself testifies with our spirit
that we are God's children. Now if we are chil-
dren, then we are heirs—heirs of God and co-heirs
with Christ, if indeed we share in his sufferings
in order that we may also share in his glory.

What on earth does it mean to be co-heirs with Christ?
To share in His glory?

As they say, inquiring minds want to know. And I
needed to know *desperately.*

Seek and Find

If you are standing on the outside of a prison, you are
only mildly concerned about how one might be able to get
out. But if you are the person being held inside the prison,
you don't just casually care to know, you *desperately need* to
know so that you can escape the dungeon and breathe the
fresh air of freedom. It is an all-consuming, life or death
endeavor.

So it was with me. I inquired of the Lord. I begged Him
to teach me, show me, reveal to me, help me figure out
what He was up to. What was the original intent of the
designer?

Please, tell me who I am. What were you thinking, when
you thought of me?

Really, what is the point? Making babies? Pretending
to be Barbie® at 40? Wearing the nurse, sex kitten, house
maid, and nanny uniforms all at the same time?

Or worse, being a sweet *quiet* Christian lady? I mean no disrespect. I am so good with my sweet quiet Christian sisters. But that's not my color. I am not their color. We are all different and neither of us are *wrong* because we are different colors, unique expressions of God.

What was I to do? All through the Scriptures the Lord tells us to seek Him, search for wisdom, ask for wisdom, look for understanding as if looking for treasure. Jesus said, "Knock and it shall be opened to you, ask and it shall be given to you." (Matthew 7:7-8) So it was no surprise that the Lord began speaking, in lots of places.

It began with the *Silence of Adam* by Larry Crabb. Then John Eldrige gave beautiful insight in his book *Wild at Heart*. The Lord used these books, and others, as pieces of my own puzzle. Eldrige ventured to say that there was more to us than we *dared believe*. It was water to my parched soul.

Weight of Glory by CS Lewis took the notion even further.

> *It is possible for each to think too much of his own potential glory hereafter; it is hardly possible for him to think too often or too deeply about that of his neighbour. The load or weight, or burden of my neighbour's glory should be laid on my back, a load so heavy that only humility can carry it, and the backs of the proud will be broken. It is a serious thing to live in a society of possible gods and goddesses to remember that the dullest and most uninteresting person you talk to may one day be a creature which, if you saw it now, you would be strongly tempted to worship, or else a horror and a corruption such as you now meet, if at all, only in a nightmare. All day long we are, in some degree, helping each other to one or other of these destinations." (pgs. 45, 46)*

Then the Lord brought writings from Watchman Nee.

They stirred up a spiritual hornet's nest, buzzing around all that I had believed about myself and God.

> *In Romans 3:23 we read "All have sinned and*
> *fall short of the glory of God."*
> *God's purpose for man was glory, but sin*
> *thwarted that purpose by causing man to miss*
> *God's glory.*
> *When we think of sin, we instinctively think of*
> *the judgment it brings; we invariably associate it*
> *with condemnation and hell.*
> *Man's thought is always of the punishment that*
> *will come to him if he sins.*
> *But God's thought is always of the Glory man*
> *will miss if he sins.*
> *The result of sin is that we forfeit God's glory.*
> *The result of redemption is that we are*
> *qualified again for glory.*
> *God's purpose in redemption is*
> *Glory.*
> *Glory.*
> *Glory.*

> *Watchman Nee*
> The Normal Christian Life *page 104*

And if these sources weren't enough, God's word itself was speaking. Loudly. Boldly.
Even Brazenly.
Glory.

> *But whenever anyone turns to the Lord, the veil*
> *is taken away.*
> *Now the Lord is the Spirit, and where the Spirit*
> *of the Lord is, there is freedom.*
> *And we, who with unveiled faces all reflect the*
> *Lord's glory, are being transformed into his like-*
> *ness with ever-increasing glory, which comes*
> *from the Lord, who is the Spirit.*
> *(2 Corinthians 3:16 -18)*

"Arise shine for your light has come.
And the glory of the Lord has risen upon you." (Isaiah 60:1)

Me? Glory? Are you kidding?

The Lord kept bringing truth to my soul. From the word, from books, from leaders. Then came a pure gift of love. I read *Waking the Dead* by John Eldrige and prayed a simple prayer.

God I want my heart back, my whole heart.

39 – whole heart

You know as well as I do that it was not the book but the prayer. You know also it could have happened in a moment. Instead the Lord chose to take me back to the places where I lost it. Rejection, denial, anger, jealousy. Any of those bus stops sound familiar?

The Lord used this journey, the "scenic" route I had traveled, to birth a whole new understanding of what a woman is and is not, who she is and is not, because of who He is and is not.

The Eldrige book woke something in my spirit that had been brooding there. Not the church line that we are all His daughters and we serve and strive to be good little church ladies…but that me, Jana, was a wonder to the God who made me. But how do I get there? How do I get OUT? I wanted out of the molds, the boxes. I wanted to just be me.

Over time the Lord kept whispering a vision, a calling, a hope of Jana. The Real Jana. Not the sick, broken, sinful Jana. Rather the Jana that God thought of when He thought of me before time began. The Jana that was waiting to be released from a hunk of stone, like Michelangelo releasing David. I wanted the Lord to chip off, chisel away anything that didn't look like His glory in me.

Go read Psalm 139 again.

It is astounding to think that God thinks of us more often than there are grains of sand in the ocean. Do we really get that He knit us together? He made us. He loves us.

He made you. He loves you. *Completely*. Right now.

I have heard it said that when we lose sight of God we lose sight of the value of life. We then lose sight of the wonder of creation, and thus lose sight of the majesty of the Creator. The more we try to conform to each other and try to be the same, the more we miss out on the beauty of our God. The more we miss out on the beauty of our God, the more we miss out on *our beauty* as an expression *of Him.*

It works the other way around as well. The more I read my Bible, the bigger God gets. The more I see what He wants to do with and through His children, the more I see how He wants relationship rather than duty. Freedom more than boxes.

The more I understood freedom from God's perspective, the easier it was to push out of the boxes that had enclosed me. Instead of walls, there was His glory as my glory. Beauty for ashes.

Chuck and I have been in John Dee's class for over five years now. I went there totally broken in heart and spirit and starving to death spiritually. John's message impacted me eternally. He taught the truth about how God changes people over time, the truth that God likes me, and he's not mad at me. The truth that I am the bride of Christ, despite all my frailties, and that He is really proud of me. The truth that He is a person, "who made everything, who lacks nothing, yet craves relationship with me." I was astounded. Late one night I got up and poured out what I thought God had poured into my soul:

How can you run after me
As unlovely as I am
How can you delight in me
when I'm so far from the mark?
Here I stand before you
Naked and exposed
And all I see in your eyes
Is the love you long to show

How can it be
You long to love me
Yearn to be near me
resting in my garden

How can it be?
You hunger for me
Yearn to be near me
enjoying my beauty
What absurdity
that such majesty
desires this humble heart
Oh Lord I am only beautiful
because my heart reflects your love.

This poem sat in the quiet space of my heart and my computer for months. Brooding, until my heart was ready to take it on. I happened to find it one day as I was working on songs for a worship CD. I sat there amazed. Where did this come from?

As I began working on the melody the Lord told me the song wasn't done. So together we wrote the second verse.

How can you sing over me
You believe in who I am
How can you dance over me.
You see more than what I can
Here I stand before you
simply overwhelmed
that though I'm far from finished
I have charmed you once again
How can it be
You long to love me
Yearn to be near me
resting in my garden
How can it be
You hunger for me
yearn to be near me
enjoying my beauty.

Such extravagance
that your loving glance
would favor this lowly face
Oh Lord I'm only beautiful
because my heart reflects your love
Oh Lord you think I'm beautiful
and my heart returns your love.

God is beautiful. "And we, with unveiled faces all reflect the glory of God." It's about His glory. I reflect His glory. He did that on purpose. Why would He do that?

Because He really likes me. A lot. He wants His glory in me to be unleashed.

Unhindered.

The same is true about you.

You reflect His glory. He really *likes you*. He wants His glory in you unhindered.

And remember, God is unstoppable.

This may stretch you a bit, but have you ever considered that we dismiss His glory when we try to be something we are not? God is far bigger than we give Him credit for. He is expansive. He is ultimate creativity. He is unique in every possible way. Therefore, His glory is reflected in us like a palette of colors. But we try to live in a black and white world. When we try to fit in little church molds, or Hollywood molds, as cookie-cutter women looking mostly the same, we say in essence: God is pretty boring, standard, conforming.

God is *trans*forming. Restoring.

My invitation is for you to bang on the *women walls* with me. Let's break out of the boxes. Why? Because I think we've been given more than we've dared to take hold of. "Not that I have already obtained all this, or have already been made perfect, but I press on to take hold of that for which Christ Jesus took hold of me." (Philippians 3:12-13)

Remember the promised land? God instructed the Israelites to "take possession" of the land He had given them. When they did not, it cost them 40 years in the desert.

What have you taken hold of? What do you press on toward?

All that Christ has to offer?

Or a toned-down practical vision of your own?

Maybe the better question is what are you settling for?

Here is a part of an email conversation that I exchanged with a dear friend when Chuck and I were at a relational impasse.

The fight was not about "submission". But it is my experience that the answer to any relational conflict is for a woman to "get back into submission."

I was explaining that I had *heard* from the Lord and would *hold onto* the Lord until Chuck came around. My over-arching premise was that God had placed a calling on my life and that this calling was equal to the call of being a wife and mother.

I love being a wife. I love being a mom. But first, I love Jesus. I believe God is calling and has equipped women for more than we are comfortable with. This premise did not settle too well with some of my Christian sisters. This is a portion of one response I received.

> *I sensed some bitterness when we were talking earlier about "submission." I know that submission isn't exactly the issue, but I felt that God brought to mind the following section from Lies Women Believe and the Truth that sets them free by Nancy Leigh DeMoss:*
> *In the past couple of decades, there has been a significant movement challenging men to become men of God, to love their wives and children, and to express that love through sacrifice and service. What an encouragement it has been to see God stirring men and turning their hearts toward Him and toward their homes. However, in the midst of this emphasis, we women need to be careful that we do not lose sight of the primary roles God has given us to fulfill. In today's evangelical world, it is "politically correct" to*

challenge men to go home and serve their wives. However, it is not "P.C." to talk to women about their responsibility to serve their husbands.

The truth is that God did not make the man to be a "helper" to the woman. He made the woman to be a "helper" to the man.
One of the things that strikes me most about the "virtuous woman" of Proverbs 31 is the fact that she is so utterly selfless. She is not seeking "self-fulfillment"; she isn't interested in advancing "her career", having her own bank account, or being known for her personal accomplishments. To the contrary, she seems virtually unconcerned about her own interests and needs, choosing instead to focus on how she can meet the practical needs of her husband and children, as well as others in her community.

Take a fresh look at this woman:
She is well-dressed (v. 22)

She and her family have food to eat and enough to share with others (vv. 15, 20)

She lives a well-ordered life; she is emotionally stable and free from fear about the future (vv. 21, 25)

Her husband is crazy about her - he is faithful to her, he feels she is "one in a million" and tells her so, and he brags about her to his friends (vv. 11, 28-29, 31)

Her children honor and praise her (v. 28)

How did she get all those "benefits"? By making it her number one priority (after her relationship with God) to meet the needs of her family.

This friend loves me deeply and I love her deeply. We have walked together for a long time.

However.

This one email summed up the poor teaching I had been given about women for 13 years in the church. There are many points in the book she referenced I agree with, but this trite and selective breakdown of the Proverbs 31 model really fired me up. Go back and read all that the Proverbs 31 woman was really about. But in this book it's as if we are saying, "Let's put women in boxes. Cute, quiet little boxes. Pretty on the outside. Empty on the inside. One size better fit all dearie, because unfortunately there's only one size."

And then, girlfriends, let's be really, really happy about the identical little boxes that we have been put in. Let's grit our teeth and smile and be *pretty*. And empty.

I am being sarcastic of course but this just can't be the "life abundantly" Jesus promised. No way.

It took a lot of guts for my friend to send that email. I love her for it. But it just doesn't add up. This harkens back to the two lines of Christian thought that 1) women should find their sole enjoyment and function from being a wife and mother, and 2) that we are to meet men's needs regardless of our own. This does not sound like co-heirs to me. This does not sound like mutual submission. This sounds like a dolled-up prison.

And heaven forbid...what if you are single? How then do you find fulfillment? Is there a big neon sign on your forehead that reads: no man = no worth?

I don't think so. I don't think this is the original intent of our loving designer.

Here is my response to my friend's well-meaning email. I'll dissect it a bit more at the end.

> *Thanks so much for your time and heart to send*
> *this. I know that it is very hard for you to send*
> *and hard for me to speak about.*
> *Can we talk about this? I want you to know how*

much I care about this topic and issue not only in my own marriage but in the Church in general.

Because the word "Help Meet" does not mean "Help Mate." It does not mean helper in the sense that the modern church likes to teach. The Proverbs 31 woman was a business woman trading and selling fields. She was far more than this and many other descriptions that make us only pretty little cookie cutter and worn out Christian women. In a book by a man no less...Discovering the Mind of a Woman, author Ken Nair talks about how together and only together, we reflect the image of God in ways not possible alone. The woman was not given so she could be an ornament, care for children (there weren't any) and clean the house (they didn't have one). But that God gave her to teach the man about relationships. The man takes his strength and creates a safe protected place that she might thrive and pour out all that God has given for the Man, herself, and the family to come. It is an awesome book and Chuck and I have been really blessed by it.
In short, we are co-heirs with Christ. It is not heresy to say that God has called me and called us to a greater vision. It is not heresy to ask God to bring to fruition all that he has promised.
It is okay to be a wife and mother fully, and still follow hard after God and his purposes.
I heard this going awry with you and that's why I wanted to talk more with you. It is too easy to say, Well if Jana would stay home more and do X, Y, Z, then Chuck would be healthy and happy.

I don't think so. Chuck needs more of Jesus, not more of Jana.
Thank you for interceding for me. I am taking

this back to Lord.
The heart of what I was trying to say is that
somehow the Lord has a purpose and timing. My
job is to lay everything down in the Lord's hands
and pick it up when he gives me leave. Usually
that involves Chuck's blessing. But not always.

The Lord is still my Lord. Not Chuck.

This may sound crazy or even harsh. But I share this
because there are lots of crazy ideas about what a woman
is supposed to do and be, or *not* supposed to do and be.
Chuck and I did resolve our dispute.

The Lord changed both our hearts through a holy
compromise. This is a pattern of how we do marriage. We
believe that Jesus brings peace and harmony when he is
being rightly exalted.

We both have voices. We both speak and listen. And if
there is an impasse — we wait. We wait on our spiritual
leader, Jesus, to bring us to unity. One or both of our hearts
are changed by Him, so that we can walk together, side by
side, strength to strength. I know many, many marriages
where this scenario would seem absurd. But when I look
at the Bible, and I look at God, there are mountains of
evidence that suggest there is much, much more to our
original design.

But before I go there, let me address the huge elephant
sitting between us right now called *submission.*

The Elephant on Our Heads

I am in favor of submission. But I am in favor of
submission Jesus-style. That often looks very different
from submission church-style. Here is where I stand on
this issue. I will share my reasoning and research with you
later on.

Some views on female submission take about five verses
from the Bible and try to tell women what they can and
cannot do. These often-cited verses may or may not be in

context. However, I believe the *whole* counsel of God, the entire Bible, is useful for teaching, correction, rebuke and training in godliness, as Timothy says. I think the *whole* Bible applies to women as well as to men.

As I read the Bible, it seems obvious that God's number one goal is relationship and His second goal is that you and I conform to the image of Christ. How strange to hear then, most sermons about women being about submission. It's as if some pastors are saying the Bible's algebraic equation is "woman equals submission." The Bible does not say that. Not at all.

As I have gone back to the Lord over this very issue in marriage, one very important distinction surfaced. See if you can find it in this passage:

> **Wives**, *submit to your husbands as to the Lord. For the husband is the head of the wife as Christ is the head of the church, his body, of which He is the Savior. Now as the church submits to Christ, so also wives should submit to their husbands in everything.*
>
> **Husbands**, *love your wives, just as Christ loved the church and gave himself up for her to make her holy, cleansing her by the washing with water through the word, and to present her to himself as a radiant church, without stain or wrinkle or any other blemish, but holy and blameless. In this same way, husbands ought to love their wives as their own bodies.*
> (Ephesians 5: 22-28)

Did you catch it? I tried to give you a hint. It is so obvious we miss it every time. The Lord is the person talking to wives about submission. He never tells the *men* to tell the *women* about submission. He will do that himself. Likewise, the Lord never tells the *women* to tell the *men* how to love them like Christ.

He will do that.

He is the only person who can do that with a pure heart,

with completely pure motives.

But it is the strangest thing. Men love to talk about submission. Can you believe the subject of women's submission came up at my husband's *sales* meeting at work recently? How weird is that? When the topic was mentioned the men all nodded knowingly, shaking their heads mumbling, that's right, that's right, women ought to submit.

But my ever-clever husband, whom God has so gifted in this area, responded with a not-so-popular perspective. He told them that women were instructed to submit to their husbands but men were instructed to love their wives as Christ loved the church. He said, "Guys, if we were to get a report card on who was doing better, women submitting to their husbands or men loving their wives like Christ, who do you think would get the better grade?"

There was an odd silence around the room. Chuck is my rock star.

When we talk about submission let's include all the verses from Ephesians.

How about *submit to* **one another** *out of reverence* **for Christ**. Where is that you ask? It is the *first* instruction about submission, right *before* the specific instructions given to the sexes. The piece of the submission puzzle that always seems to be missing is the Jesus piece.

Submit to your husband as *unto the Lord*, the Bible instructs women.

Love your wives just as *Christ loved the church*, the Bible instructs men.

I think perhaps we miss this distinction because we don't know or don't dare to love as Christ loves. Christ said His yoke was easy and His burden light. (Matthew 11:28) Who would not want to submit, or "come up under" that kind of care? But male authority apart from Christ is heavy and burdensome and imprisoning. I think we have missed the mark because we have missed the original design.

It is not about role, it is about identity. God wants us *both* to be fully engaged with *Him* and then fully engaged with each other. He desires both to thrive in His original design, the two images being perfect reflections of Him. Yes we have different strengths and weaknesses but God uses those to help us look more like Jesus.

Something More

You may be tempted to think because of the journey Chuck and I have been on that somehow this issue is out of whack for us. On the contrary, in spite of the heartache in some areas of our married life, Chuck has been an outstanding warrior for me. He knows, and has known, my heart well enough to know I could not *thrive* if he pushed me around or demanded to be boss. Instead he modeled Christ in that he *invited* me to join him. He has, particularly in recent years, encouraged my gifts and callings and my walk with Jesus. Chuck's goal has been to empower me. He has earned my respect. I could give many examples but one sticks out in my mind.

As a new Christian, I needed to get baptized, again. This time for real. Chuck had a heavy concern for this. But instead of playing some "submission" card and telling me that I had to because *he said so*, he prayed for me and gently asked me about it every three months or so.

You see, Chuck knew my heart and the hurt and skepticism about empty ritual. Had he demanded my action out of blind duty, he would have been guilty of causing me to repeat the same cycle. But he did not. He prayed and reminded gently.

What happened?

One day I turned on the radio and Andy Stanley said, "Let's talk about baptism." I sat down on the couch and listened. A half hour later, I felt like Jesus and I had had this great conversation about all I had misunderstood about baptism and why it was important.

I called Chuck right away. "I've got to get baptized!" I said, laughing.

That is loving your wife as Christ loved the church. Working for her good. Even Christ never demanded His own way but did only what His Father directed.

You know, I never *once* heard Jesus tell anyone to *submit*.

Let me tell you what I am not:

I am not a feminist. I love God-empowered women. I equally love God-empowered men. I think men *and women* are made in the image of God. I like my man, I need my man. I don't have to diminish my man to be a God-style woman.

I am not a supermom. I have never seen full time careers and families mix well. Someone always pays and it is usually the people who need us the most, our children.

I am incredibly grateful for a redeemed life and family. The Lord is healing the wounds in my marriage. I love Chuck. He has hurt me more than anyone. But he has blessed me more than anyone. I have learned so much from him. In addition, one of my dearest delights is my children. I love my family. For the record, I am a stay-at-home wife and mom.

By choice and by sacrifice.

But...

I have another calling too.

I am a woman of God *first*. He is my *first* relationship. *God* is first.

When God calls me to do something, I listen. I remind Him, not that He needs to be reminded of anything, but I remind Him that I have a family. I ask Him to help me balance all that He is calling forth. And you know what? — He does. If I stay aligned with Him, he works out the details. He fills in the gaps.

Romans 11:29 says "for the gifts and the calling of God are irrevocable." It is His job to equip and sustain those He has gifted and called. But it is also His choice and decision about *who* is gifted and *who* is called.

All through the Bible and history, you see that God is not limited in His expressions of women or His anointing of women. Think of some the women's names in the Bible, they are all very different kinds of women: Abigail, Mary, Ruth, Esther, Deborah, Priscilla, Miriam, Martha.

Do you see? Even in the Scriptures there are many colors of women. Reserved, loud. Warrior, subtle. Gentle, bold. Tender, piercing.

Let me think a minute, who does that remind me of?

Oh that's right, all those sound like descriptions, or images, of Jesus.

Here are a few current-day women I know:

My friend Christie has four children. Her calling and gifting is to be a great homemaker. She also teaches a co-ed Sunday school class. She does not work outside the home.

My friend Donna is a single woman who adopted a little girl from Kazakhstan. She works full time to support them.

My friend Danna is very quiet and orderly. She and her husband adopted two sons from the Philippines. She works part time from her home.

My friend Debbie is single woman who runs her own business and cares for her two aging parents.

I could not carry the burden that any of these women carry. I do not have God's anointing to do any of their callings. I look at them with awe and respect. We are all so different. Yet we're all on track with where God is taking us as women. A palette of God colors.

But when we are not allowed to thrive and live in our true colors, we suffer. Do you see, just maybe, why we as women whine or get depressed or go shopping? Because when we get put into boxes, we slam against walls.

Let me give you a few phrases about women and see if they fit any of your female experiences:

She is so aggressive.

She is so scatter-brained.

What a weak-willed woman.

What a strong-willed woman. (Odd that both weak and strong is criticized…)

Women *should be* content to stay at home.

Women need to work to carry the load.

Why does my wife think she can tell me what to do?

Cleaning the house is her job.

You're just a silly girl.

A woman needs to know her place.

These are all true-to-life comments made to or about women I know. Each has a venom of its own. Let me summarize my thoughts by answering the very last phrase: a woman needs to know her place.

There are lots of crazy definitions of a woman. My definition starts with Jesus. When we as women know that our place is in the embrace of Jesus, it changes everything about how we view ourselves, our world and even our men.

40 — back to the beginning

There is a story that has been started by God. A love story. A wild reckless adventure. A tense and thrilling romance. A high-action chase scene through the streets of the world. The ultimate whodunit.

It begins in the garden. You probably know this passage, just like I thought I did. But let me point out a few key phrases that may have slipped your notice.

> *Then God said, "Let us make man in our image, in our likeness,* **and let them rule** *over the fish of the sea and the birds of the air, over the livestock, over all the earth, and over all the creatures that move along the ground." So God created man in his own image, in the image of God he created him; male and female he created them. (Genesis 1:26-27)*

But have you ever noticed the four little words, "and let *them* rule…"

Funny that. Never seem to hear about that in church. Not from a *role* perspective but from a *God* perspective. From the beginning He has been up to something, He has been telling a story that needed both sexes fully engaged, fully released in a living relationship with their maker and fully engaged with each other. Instead we play word games about who is to do what.

How petty. God is setting the stage for an amazing work, and we are talking about who empties the dishwasher.

There are those who would say that creating the woman was an after-thought. As if God would say, "Oopsy! We forgot something." There are those who would say that no suitable helper was found, so we need to make Adam a woman so she can cook and clean and have babies and give sex. I can't tell you how many Christian books spread some version of the suitable helper idea.

However, Ken Nair beautifully dispels this myth in his outstanding book, *Discovering the Mind of a Woman.*

> *"The idea that women are inferior, or less than men, is too often substantiated in Christian circles by the current misuse of a particular word found in Genesis 2:18. That word is help meet. In the King James Version, God is quoted as saying, 'I will make him a help meet.' Unfortunately, the word help meet has been wrongly reclassified, re-interpreted, and rephrased. We are taught today that the word is helpmate. And generations of Bible teachers have continued with that misinformation, teaching that women are helpmates...*
>
> *When I ask men what they think would be reasonable working definition for the title help meet (even though I used help meet, their frame of reference is helpmate), here's what I usually hear: "Someone whose job it is to rear the children, do the housekeeping, the laundry, and the dishes."*
>
> *Trying to explain how that thinking is a distortion of God's reason for inventing a helper, I follow my questions with this line of reasoning: "to get a better idea of the purposes God had in mind when He invented women let's go back to the beginning of time. Let's imagine God has just finished creating woman and had named her 'helper.' Were there any children?*
>
> *The guy says, "No."*

Were there any houses?
Again, "No."
Were they any clothes to launder?
"No."
Any dishes to do?
"No."
That being the case, isn't it reasonable to con-
clude that we should eliminate those activities as
her purpose behind the title helper or help meet?
(pages 37-39)

Nair goes on to explain how God knew the extensiveness of sin's separation and He knew that Adam would need help in the journey of godliness. Instead of woman being a tool to be used by the man to fill all manner of selfish desires, Nair suggests God is giving man an immeasurable gift.

"This helper will provide you with a means
of measuring whether or not you are becom-
ing more and more like what I want you to be,
spiritually alive and functional. Christ is your
example and the way. Then as you become more
Christ-like you will also be furnishing your wife
with the leadership that proves an example worth
following. Together you re-establish the spirit-to-
spirit relationship that was lost."

Finally, Nair challenges men, and I want to challenge us as women, to consider women "as equals — partners with God, whose God-given purpose is to help us discover the differences between the standard male attitudes in our hearts and Christlike attitudes."

Do you hear the inspiration for both the man and the woman to live in their strength and their beauty? In this environment both are equally dependent on Jesus for revelation and empowering and sustenance. Each has a voice and respects the other image of God. Now place these mutually honoring ideas next this pastor's comments.

A Skewed View

At a marriage retreat a senior pastor stated in his opening comments:

"Ladies let me just tell you right off the bat that the answer to everything is sex. Every question you came here with, the answer is sex. Right men?" While the women gasped in disbelief, the men laughed nervously.

Chuck gently covered my hand with his as I held the table in a death grip. Then we waited. The whole room waited for the punch line from the pastor. We kept hoping to hear, "Nah I'm just kidding" or "seriously let's get down to business."

Anything, anything that would reverse the burden he had just placed on already weary women. Unfortunately, instead of a reversal, we had to sit through the next two sessions explaining why that was indeed the cold hard fact. We were told, girls just give it up. Submit. It's your duty.

This does not sound like the God I know.

When it was my turn to teach and I had the women alone for my session I asked them:

Do you believe that sex is the answer to everything?

Their overwhelming response was "No!".

I pressed further and asked them about the garden. Do you think that the God of the universe who has made all this beauty and magnificence, the big and the small, with great detail and delight, missed something? Do you think this same God who spoke into being everything in the earth, except for man, and the man He formed with His own hand out of the dust, do you think this God dropped the ball?

Remember now, this God wanted contact with Adam so much that with His own breath He breathed life into him. Do you think when God stood back to survey all that He made, He looked at Adam and gasped at the sight of his — penis? Did God think "Oh my, what am I going to do about that? He will never get anything done, I better make him a woman."

It may be funny. But it is also ridiculous to think and live as if that were so.

Rather it is confirmation that the woman is a completer. She is the rest of the puzzle. Or should I say image? Read this passage out of Genesis 5.

> *In the day that God created man, in the likeness of God made he him. Male and female created he them; and blessed them, and called their name Adam, in the day when they were created. (Genesis 5:1a-2)*

Now that's odd. My whole life in church and out of church, I have never heard a message preached on this point. And called **their name Adam**. Together, male and female they were created in the image of the living God. He named them. And they shared one name.

Let that soak in for a minute. This truth was profound for me. Because woman is not bound to the kitchen, or the bedroom. She is a co-ruler with her man. Both of their strengths were blessed by God. Both of them were given His image, to reflect Him differently for sure. But there is no *thought* of him better or her better. They are both uniquely made and uniquely gifted. And wholly loved by their Creator.

Genesis 2: 20 reads that there is no help meet for the man. So the Lord took a rib from his side and fashioned woman and brought her to him. He exclaimed, "This is now bone of my bones and flesh of my flesh; and she shall be called woman, for she was taken out of man."

Now notice the two footnotes in my NIV Bible.

Gen. 2:7
The Hebrew for man (adam) sounds like and may
be related to the Hebrew for ground (adamah); it
is also the name *Adam (see <u>Gen. 2:20</u>).*

Gen. 2:23
The Hebrew for woman sounds like the
Hebrew for man.

Am I saying that women and men are the same? I am not. However it is profound that they shared ruling, they shared a name, they shared God's image. Our pastor, Rick Dunn, once remarked that God reached in near the heart of man and pulled out the "other face of God hidden there." I love that, the other *face* of God.

God made her separate and yet a part of him.

Unique but unified.

One but individuals.

Two ruling together as one.

God was not finished, he did not *rest*, until both the man and the woman were made. They walked with their maker, and made love in the presence of their maker, and they found unity and trust and relationship with no interruption.

The man and woman were both naked and they felt no shame.

Remember, shame means to take away honor. Dis-honor. It is "a painful emotion resulting from an awareness of inadequacy" says a web dictionary. But in the garden there was *no* shame...No awareness of anything lacking.

No "less than."

In the garden there was honor. There was fullness. There was freedom, peace, and trust. There was selfless love. There was intimacy, with each other and with their Maker. Talk about paradise. No wonder we yearn for that kind of relationship.

So then where does the idea of the man as the boss come from?

Where does the idea of women clawing after the men come from?

Let's keep reading. The evil one started asking questions. Instead of all the one billion things man and woman, Adam and Adam, could have done, they just stood there. The woman tried to play word games. Adam, "her husband, who was with her," did nothing. (Genesis 3:7)

Several authors, Larry Crabb in *The Silence of Adam*, Ken Nair and others breathed truth into the "woman is the problem" philosophy I had heard for so long.

Together they ruled and together they fell. One bite, one thought of doubt, one tree and all was lost. All that they had known as perfection. Gone. They are in a flash very, very aware of all that they are now lacking.

If this is not bad enough, then comes the curse. Read this carefully.

Your desire will be for your husband,
and he will rule over you. (Genesis 3:16)

I think no one felt the curse more deeply than Adam and the newly named Eve. They fell from complete wholeness and unhindered relationship into groveling and wrestling for fulfillment and power. They were dis-honored. Shamed. Now, they were lacking. In a moment they knew selfishness and fighting over being right. In a flash they knew isolation and lying and hiding. Betrayal. Even the fact that Adam named her, a sign of separation, was after the curse.

I remember as a new Christian doing a Bible study with a dear sister who tried to show me this passage to convince me to "submit" to my husband.

"See," she said, "it says right here that he will rule over you. This is the model for us to follow."

Its part of the CURSE! I sputtered back.

I was too young in faith and the Word to understand why that didn't fit. Now after many years of walking with the Lord, I am beginning to have a glimmer of understanding.

Desire and Power

Let's start with the women: *your desire will be for your husband.*

When I see women constantly trying to catch a man's eye, trying to please him at all costs, doing whatever it takes to get a man or keep a man, you can pretty much bet that she is living under the curse. Instead of living out of the image of God, she is living out of what I call "the *False Woman*," the *what do you want me to be,* curse. Her thought is ever on herself and how to get or keep the illusive man. He becomes her god. She seeks his approval rather than standing in freedom as the woman image of God she has been created to be. She lives cowering in man's shadow.

Okay now it's the guys' turn: *and he will rule over her.*

Man and woman were co-rulers. But when sin entered the picture there is the fight for dominance. But it is not from the woman. When you see or hear a guy talking about putting her in her place, calling the shots, telling the little woman how it is, laying down the law, you can pretty much bet that he is living under the curse. Men love power.

In some marriages I know, the man has taken on the notion that being a "leader" means being "Dad's in charge" with sexual perks from his wife. The same woman who captured her husband's heart and mind with her wit and wisdom now needs to be told when to get up, when to clean the house, when to do the laundry. It is amazing to me that we call this manhood.

I often hear men preachers and teachers say that women want to rule their husbands. That is not what Scripture says. And if you look closely it is not what is lived out in most relationships. Actually it is quite the opposite.

It says her *desire* will be for her husband.

This word 'desire' is intense longing. Grasping.

Women claw after men to get their needs met. Meaning, her desire, her passion, her focus, her energy will be wrongly placed on the whims and wiles of the man. She will do whatever it takes to get his attention and keep his attention. For this very reason, I hate the Disney movie *The Little Mermaid*. The main character Ariel will do anything, even abandoning her true self as a mermaid, to be with the man. It is the grasping, clawing, "I'll be whatever you want me to be" curse.

Eve once had complete fulfillment in God's presence and in co-ruling with the man, Adam. But then she lost both. She became separated from her God, and her husband totally discredits her. From then on her focus was on making life work according to her abilities to woo and seduce. It's a very grave curse. Her legacy to us feels as if we have our true image of God trapped in a hunk of stone. Instead of being women who are fulfilled by God, known and appreciated by man, we run and grasp after fulfillment from men. Please love me, no matter what, is our heart's cry.

She grasps for attention any way she can get it, and the man's first tendency is to dismiss her. He will rule over her. Men want the power of telling women yes or no. Sit or stay. For all the accusations of women wanting power, that is *his* curse. He wants to be boss. Her curse is she wants to be *everything* he ever wanted.

True Desire

A friend of mine came to visit after a disturbing message at her church. She said the pastor used the Genesis curse to say that "your desire will be for your husband" meant that women would want to control and manipulate men. This really bothered her. And me too.

As I was researching the meaning of word *desire* the Lord revealed a whole other truth about *His love* for us.

This is amazing.

Look at the cross-reference verse used to describe this *desire*, this aching.

"I am my beloved's and *his desire* is toward *me*" (Song of Songs 7:10)

This is the same "desire" from Genesis. It struck me as so bizarre. Of all the interpretations frequently used to describe the curse of the woman's desire, with most of them saying it means that she fights for power, I have never heard this Scripture cited.

Do you know what women want more than anything?

(Control! the men shout. Nope.)

She longs for adoration. For pure desire. Being enthralled with her and only her. To be the One of ones. To be fully realized and known and appreciated. Why would that be part of the curse?

Because that's how it was before the fall. Before the fall she was full of the knowledge of God, full of the companionship with man, fully complete. Dare I say it, could it be that on that side of the fall, Adam and Eve had no need. They were full.

And now the woman is craving, empty, longing, aching. Remember the haunting from the first chapters? You could thank our mother Eve for that legacy.

But on the other hand, stop and consider what this could possibly mean — God has this kind of strong desire for me.

For you.

"I am my beloved's and his *desire* is toward me"
(Song of Songs 7:10)

Have you ever considered that God aches for you, the way you ache for a man?

This is why being freed from the curse is so critical to our hearts. We were made for desire. Because we were made in the *image* of a God of desire.

And He longs to fill our desire.

Men and women place all this need and weight on each other when they live out of the curse. Her desire is for him, his desire is to rule. They both fail because neither were created to meet this "need" in the other.

No wonder this is a sick relational cycle.

Before you get too depressed let me tell you the good news. Contrary to popular opinions, if you call Jesus your Lord like I do, then we no longer live under the curse. Even in the garden there was hope.

Jesus came to restore the blessing. He came to destroy the efforts of the devil and break the yoke of the curse.

There is a much more to us than scraping for the man's attention. Much more to marriage than bickering about who is the boss. There is more of Jesus in us than we can possibly bear.

Have you ever considered that the point of the cross and resurrection was to un-do the curse? What was done in the first Adam was overcome by Christ.

"For if the many died by the trespass of the one man, how much more did God's grace and the gift that came by the grace of the one man, Jesus Christ, overflow to the many!" (Romans 5:15)

Instead of men exerting strength to dominate women, instead of women clawing at men to get their needs met, we "too may have new life." (Romans 6:4)

But what is new life for a woman? Too many times, our perception of women is twisted. Take Grumpy, one of the Seven Dwarves. He was pretty adamant when they found Snow White asleep. While the other dwarves looked on in admiration of her beauty and angelic features, Grumpy set the record straight.

"Angel? hah! She's a female. And all females [is] poison! They're full of womanly wiles! —

When the dwarves questioned him with "What are "womanly wiles"?

He answered in a common male fashion, "I don't know, but I'm 'agin' 'em."

Sounds like some preachers I know.

Or take the verse about the weaker sex.

> *Husbands, in the same way be considerate as you*
> *live with your wives, and treat them with respect*
> *as the weaker partner and as heirs with you of*
> *the gracious gift of life, so that nothing will hin-*
> *der your prayers. (1 Peter 3:7)*

Weaker.

What is the origin of this unusual sounding word? It comes from the Greek asthenes (weak), from a (=not) and sthenos (=strong). Balashon - *Hebrew Language Detective*

Weaker meaning *not strong*. It does not mean
— not smart, not reasonable, not able. It does not mean inadequate in any way. It means not strong. But look at the remainder of the sentence — as heirs with you of the gracious gift of life. Joint heirs...

I know men who really think women are inferior. I know churches who love and honor their women, they just don't want to *hear* from their women. That is what one of their own members said.

I know women's ministries that are run by *all male* boards. It is as if the same Godly wisdom needed to *run* the ministry is not good enough to *lead* the ministry. Equally ridiculous is an all female board. We need the Divine image as seen separately in the male and female images.

I also know women who really think that they should not tell their husbands what they think about any given issue because "he is the leader." Somehow these bright capable women prior to marriage are now to be numb and silent as they wait on their man to forge the way without their God-given insight and perspective. This is not biblical manhood or biblical womanhood. The two become one. Not the one becomes dumb and mute.

What do you do with Phoebe and Deborah, and the accurate Proverbs 31 woman? These women kicked butt.

They weren't men. They were God's *anointed* women.
It is not about them. It is about the God they loved and
gave their all to. It's about a God who made them and
has a purpose for all of His children. God certainly is not
confined to man-made boxes. He can do *whatever* He likes
through *whomever* He chooses.

There are generations of women who read God's word
and apply it to their lives because the Great Love Letter
is written equally to all people. But there is an irony here
for me. A woman can look at Joseph and King David and
Abraham, and she learns and gleans from them and tries
to model them.

But you never hear a man say, "Hey I have been studying
Proverbs 31 to see how to love my family better." Or "Have
you ever looked at Mary and Martha? Those chicks knew
how to be in relationship with Jesus, I have learned so
much reading about them."

Do you get it?

I am not raising either sex above the other. Why?
Because it is all level ground at the cross. Do you hear that?
Level ground at the cross. The whole counsel of God is for
us all. His Spirit is working in us all. For the glory of God.

How about we strive to love Jesus and let Him pour out
in whatever fashion and through whomever He desires?

What Did Jesus Do?

Dr. Hagar wrote *As Jesus Cared for Women* and through
that book he really flushed out some lies in my belief
system. It was so refreshing to read the heart of a man who
saw that Jesus didn't look down on women. He loved them,
restored them, elevated them, honored them, listened to
them. Jesus didn't try to put them in boxes. Jesus wanted
them to be free.

He didn't die so that they might be discounted and
discredited as the weaker sex. He died to release them
from the curse, from spending all their energy running
after a man or from being ruled by one.

He died so His women would be *free* to love *Him*, fully.

Have you ever considered how Jesus radically rocked the world in His treatment of women?

–The adulteress He forgave. But He looked down at the ground, instead of cruising her.

–The Samaritan woman He asked for water. He *asked* of her. That in itself was a gift, to interact with her as a capable equal rather than someone to be shunned. He offered her abundance instead of judgment.

–To the sinner who washed His feet with her hair, He defended her devotion in public and declared that what she had done for Him would be told for all eternity.

To Martha, He *first* revealed that He was the Resurrection.

To Mary, He *first* appeared as the Risen Lord.

Is it possible that Jesus forgot that women were property? Forgot that the weaker sex was to stay behind a man?

Or did Jesus purposely turn the male order on its ear? Did Jesus clearly become the only man she was to stand behind? Her one true spiritual leader.

I went to a wedding the other day that really laid it on thick about the husband being the spiritual leader. I wanted to get up and leave, but I fumed instead.

I came home and tried to find that in the Bible. I did a search on BlueletterBible.org. No results.

Male and female He created them, in His image He created them.

We have a Spiritual Leader. His name is Jesus.

And He is really *great* at His job.

Of all the things a man can and should be, and all the things a woman can and should be, why put on labels and pressures that we were never meant to carry?

Perhaps this side of the cross, the woman and the man are to again co-rule as co-heirs. They are to stand side by side, arm in arm, under the banner, authority and love of

Jesus Christ. Just as He said that the "two became one flesh and to let no man tear it apart," this hope of oneness lies in the power of Christ working through each face of His image. This union is about a God-created intimacy where both bring all they have to the table, male and female, and as one under Christ they live life and serve and further God's kingdom.

Do you see that when we as man and woman both live in our original intent, with our definition and desire met in our maker, then there is a *supernatural* harmony in relationship? Instead of bossing or clawing, we are both restored to walk together in our journeys with God.

Chuck and I both pour into each other, sacrifice for each other, speak truth to each other, seek counsel from each other, pray for each other. We co-rule together under the headship of Jesus Christ. We don't try to be homogeneous. We try to be authentic expressions of Jesus to each other right in the middle of our differences, strengths and weaknesses.

Why on earth does all of this matter?

Because as long as a woman is living under the curse, as long as she pours everything out trying to hook or keep a man, as long as she looks to a human man to FILL her desire, she is asking the wrong beholder to define her. She will be disappointed, dissatisfied, disillusioned. She is living out of a definition of the *False Woman*.

Because as long as a man is living under the curse, as long as he tries to rule rather than to serve and love his wife as Christ loves his wife, then he misses out on the divine gift placed right beside him in his wife. He spends his strength to be something totally different from the goal: to be like Jesus. He misses the opportunity to grow Christ-like character in his humility, patience, and endurance and the full embrace of his woman.

41 — the false woman

Let me give you an couple of illustrations of the *False Woman*.

There was a photo I got by email. The photo captures one lone woman, pale and plain, holding a sign that said, "Women are not decorations." She is glaring at the short-shorts clad women in Hooters® tank tops standing right beside her. They are bronzed, dyed and pushed up. They look at her with mocking smiles, and pity.

The only caption was "Think she is jealous?"

I looked a long, long time at that photo.

My first reaction was, no actually I am not jealous. I am *sick*. I am sick for *both* groups of women who have totally missed the point of being a woman. God's woman.

The Hooters® girl has determined that it is only what's on the *outside* that counts. She has to look "just so" to be considered a "Worthy Woman." Her success is measured by her bust size, her waist size and how many heads she turns. So much so, she is paid to turn heads. Not only does she live for that look, she is prostituting her beauty, and gets paid to let guys look down her shirt. I know, I know. Hooters® has great wings, the guys protest.

And they buy *Playboy* for the articles.

You know, I have a friend who used to work at Hooters®. And yes, she is a Christian.

She was really frustrated she couldn't find a decent guy at Hooters® who would treat her well. She went on say that

the guys didn't respect her and treated her like an object.
(Nah. Really?)

Forgive the cynicism. But the guys were only treating her as SHE treated herself.

As a woman thinks, so she is. Do you get it?

My friend is living as a *False Woman* and can't figure out why she is miserable. The *False Woman* has two faces, or two ends of the spectrum. Most of us live somewhere on the spectrum. One face, or end of the spectrum, is like the Hooters® girl. I call this obsessive desire for beauty the Trophy Woman. The other face, or spectrum end I call the Invisible Woman.

Let's revisit the email photo. The homely protesting woman has determined that it is only what's on the *inside* that counts. She has bought hook, line and sinker that it is only about "Inner Beauty." She's decided all that fluff and primp effort is vanity. Somewhere she has believed that she can't win at the beauty game, so she has quit the game altogether. Can you see her complete lack of effort is just an extreme opposite of the Trophy Woman's obsessive effort? I have found when you dig a little with the Invisible Woman, just like in the Trophy Woman, there is almost always a gaping wound.

The *Invisible Woman* wears a mantle of heartache. Her face, her countenance, her posture, screams out **un**loved, **un**attractive, **un**involved, **un**aware of God's original design of a woman. To somehow separate herself from the Trophy Woman lie, she goes to the opposite extreme.

When I talk about beauty God-style, it is not about denying it, but about *embracing* it.

In this photo you can see the pain in the protestor's eyes. Somebody somewhere told this woman that she was not lovely. And she believed that lie. When you see a woman who is **un**-tended to, I don't mean no make-up, I mean **un**-invested in, **un**-cared for, you know who I am talking about, she is living out of a definition other than her maker's.

After I taught at a single's retreat, a woman came up to me who looked very much like the Invisible Woman in this photo. I had spent two sessions explaining how God felt about her, how He had made her with precision and loved what He'd made.

She had on the pink T-shirt that I always sell at these events that says: "he's enthralled with me." It was like a new banner had been placed on her shoulders.

How are you? I asked.

She flashed a promising smile. "Better than I have been in a long time. You know when my husband left me for another woman, *eight years ago*, I think I killed that part of my heart. I haven't felt beautiful for a long time. Now I see I was asking the wrong person…"

Amen.

Whether Trophy or Invisible, both women represent the same problem from the opposite ends of the spectrum called the *False Woman*. If we don't live in God's definition then we settle for the Hollywood cultural definitions of womanhood, we let ourselves be put in assigned boxes:

Got it,

Might get it,

Used to have it,

Never had it.

We have been put in these boxes, like it or not. So when we look around the room and see all the other boxes, we have to do something to make our assigned box seem like home. So we rationalize our health, our body structure, our genes, eating patterns, our drama and trauma stories, whatever it takes, to justify the box we have been assigned to. But guess what? All of these boxes are lies.

All of them. Lies.

Run the Numbers

Lets run the math on the *False Woman* formula.

The Trophy Woman is constantly evaluating her condition. Her weight, her wrinkles, her wardrobe. (Just as a side note, she doesn't just work at Hooters®, she is sitting in the next pew.) She lives in a state of constant comparison, how is she measuring up today? She is ever-busy either giving or getting a grade. I call this *Hypersexualizing* yourself.

Hypersexualizing is when you take only the physical aspect of your womanhood and distort its purpose and focus. We are made up of many facets: heart, soul, body, spirit, dreams, emotions, beliefs. But this distorted focus takes one aspect, the body, and makes it supreme. Hypersexualized women place most of their value and worth in what the eye sees. Beauty in the eye of the beholder.

I saw this acted out in two very poignant encounters. The small group that meets at our house includes co-eds ranging from 19 to late 20s. To my knowledge there are no *dogs* attending; all of them look pretty great to me.

But you should watch the girls watch each other. One night in particular, three of us were standing in my kitchen where I have a large window. My back was to the window, while the two girls faced the window. As we talked I kept seeing them look to the window. So I would turn around to see if someone else was coming in. Seeing no one, I turned back around to return to our conversation. Again, they looked at the window, and I turned around to see also.

No one there. Back to conversation. We did this several times. I thought I must be losing my mind until one of the girls looked to the window but this time she ran her hand down her stomach and sucked in her gut. OH MY GOODNESS, I realized in a flash, they were not looking *out* the window, they were looking *in* the window at their reflection!

Before you write that off to the folly of youth, let me recount episode number two. A dear older friend of mine had gone through a serious illness. She is truly an outstanding woman and admired by all. I went to her house and we were standing in front of a large mirror just chatting. I couldn't help but notice that in a fifteen-minute conversation, she looked in the mirror and adjusted herself at least five times.

The eye of the beholder.

There is great power in the beholder. Whether we behold

with our own eyes or the eyes we attract. But I keep bringing the question back to "Whose opinion matters most?" Who is the beholder that counts?

When the outer is what mostly matters, what determines value, we miss perhaps the greater purpose of God's design. We reduce ourselves to sexual creatures, bodies for the taking. Consumer items. Great wings, great cleavage, one stop-shopping.

All you have to do is go to the store, the mall, or church, to see his eyes catch her eyes, her eyes catch his eyes. Constant little report cards going off, little connections that desperately want to know: do you like what you see?

It is not even that women communicate availability for seduction, they just simply offer their bodies as indicators of how they are stacking up for the day. They use their bodies and their clothing to try to meet the standards set by Hollywood, instead of Him.

Hypersexualizing produces a harvest of eating disorders, emotional addictions, and even sexual addictions. The drive for attempted perfection, failure to achieve perfection, and the resulting depression become a cycle that stems from us trying to be a woman that is *false*. The chicks in the magazines are not real, but we kill ourselves to try to look like them anyway. When we treat ourselves as objects, two things happen. We treat others as objects and others treat us as objects.

Remember the verse, love your neighbor as yourself. Try this on. You will love your neighbor in the same way your love yourself. Are you hard on yourself? Chances are everyone around you will say that you are hard on them too. Are you critical of yourself, your weight, your wrinkles, your wardrobe? Chances are everyone around you feels your constant critiquing of them too.

Certainly I do not advocate burlap bags and granny shoes. I believe in *expressing* our glory to the fullest extent.

But what I am talking about is the principle we established earlier in the study of Proverbs 5.

Do not let your beauty be poured out in the public square, instead your water is to be yours alone and never to be shared with strangers.

If this isn't hard enough, here is a startling passage. I felt the Lord showed it to me right before I was to teach a rather competitive group of young women who were eager to grab male attention.

The Lord says,
"The women of Zion are haughty,
walking along with outstretched necks,
flirting with their eyes,
tripping along with mincing steps,
with ornaments jingling on their ankles.

Therefore the Lord will bring sores on the heads
of the women of Zion;
the Lord will make their scalps bald."

In that day the Lord will snatch away their
finery: the bangles and headbands and crescent
necklaces,

the earrings and bracelets and veils,
the headdresses and ankle chains and sashes, the
perfume bottles and charms,
the signet rings and nose rings,
the fine robes and the capes and cloaks, the
purses
and mirrors, and the linen garments and tiaras
and shawls.

Instead of fragrance there will be a stench;
instead of a sash, a rope;
instead of well-dressed hair, baldness;
instead of fine clothing, sackcloth;
instead of beauty, branding.
(Isaiah 3:16-24)

Ouch.

So here is the rub. If God made us and thinks we are beautiful, why are we not to make our lives about being beautiful?

As with everything in the journey with Jesus, it is about our heart motive. We have one of two choices. To worship the created or the Creator. We can be led astray by the enticements around us which lead us to hypersexuality, idolatry, and despair.

Or we can follow the path of Jesus.

He said, "Love the Lord your God with all your heart and with all your soul and with all your mind and with all your strength.

The second is this: 'Love your neighbor as yourself.' There is no commandment greater than these." (Mark 12:30-31)

Never forget that God looks at the heart. When there is an understanding of *who* we are, because of *whose* we are, the game is *over*. I take care of myself because it is a way of worship, a way of saying thank you to my maker. It doesn't increase my worth. It just polishes the shine of a diamond. Of course you are beautiful. Of course I am beautiful. And, no I don't need your eyes all over my body to confirm that. I don't need your knowing smile of appreciation to make me tingle.

I knew the walls were falling one day when I pulled up to a gas station and saw the pack of males. In the past, I would have either made eye contact and smiled to draw their attention (the Trophy Woman) or I would have ducked my head in shame knowing they would not notice me (Invisible Woman).

But that day, I got out of my car looked to the sky and smiled. He delights in me, I said out loud. I nearly skipped into the store to pay for gas. I was overwhelmed by the love of the one true beholder. And the guys…

I have no idea what they did. I totally didn't care.

42 – invisible woman

The other side of the *False Woman* is the notion of *being* the ugly one.

I call this *non-sexualizing* yourself. If you can hold up a sign that says, women are not for decoration, you have taken yourself out of the game. Okay forget the sign. But you see women like this everyday. They go to school or work. Some marry. Have children. Go to church. They are great people. It's just that something is *missing*. If they only had half a face, it would make sense of how you feel in their presence. That deformity would explain why you feel there is another whole dimension to them as women that is missing. There is a part of them that they have tried to, or have been forced to, shut off. Their internal logic is: if I don't look like a woman, I won't have to feel like a woman, then you can't reject me as a woman.

We all say we don't care about all that beauty stuff, at one time or another. I think we try to convince ourselves that we don't care. But the truth is we *do* care, only we feel we can never win the beauty game. So we quit, and try to become invisible.

The *Invisible Woman* has a way of disregarding herself. Or maybe the word is dismissing. She believes she doesn't count. She feels overlooked or ignored. Even absent.

There was a young woman in our small group who consistently dressed so that her pants revealed way too much of her bottom when she sat on the floor. People tried to address it but she just blew them off. Others thought that she was flaunting her body trying to get attention. But I told them this was not the case. I had seen this before; she was displaying her body out of her faulty beliefs. In her mind she was neutral or benign or dare I say it, non-sexual. She felt very unlovely and unapproachable.

I told her gently, just because you don't like to look at you, doesn't mean men don't like to look at you. But her response is common among invisible women.

"Oh I am not the pretty one. I don't have to worry about it."

"Really? Is that what God said about you?" I told her in plain words. "You are producing sexual vibes whether you mean to or not!"

We all go through seasons of feeling a little beat up with the ugly stick…but this is different. This is a way of life. The *Invisible Woman* has come to believe she has no womanly attributes of value. She believes this so deeply that she tries to accentuate or make up for her "lacking."

My friend "Sally" is a perfect example. She told us her story once and said without blinking an eye, "I knew I wasn't pretty but I was smart. So I learned that if I could make people laugh, they would like me anyway."

I wanted to hold her and tell her what God thinks:

> *You are altogether beautiful, my darling,*
> *And there is no blemish in you.*
> *You have made my heart beat faster, my sister,*
> *my bride*
> *You have made my heart beat faster*
> *with a single glance of your eyes.*
> *(Song of Solomon 4: 7, 9)*

I am not sure she would dare to believe it. Do you?

There is a price for believing the opposite. The *Invisible Woman's* beliefs often produce bitter fruits too: eating disorders, social withdrawal, addictions, self pity.

It is a cruel irony that the *False Woman* produces the same illnesses but with different outcomes. The Trophy Woman has an eating disorder to try to stay thin and thus, hopefully, desirable. The *Invisible Woman* has an eating disorder ranging from bulimia to bingeing so she can cover her fear of rejection with pounds of comfort food. In addition, it is not uncommon for "invisible" women to be just as promiscuous as "trophy" women. Both kinds of women are trying to prove the same thing to their own hearts — I am worthy of attention, I am worth desiring.

My friend "Linda," went so far as to have surgery for her obesity. The problem is she didn't do similar life-changing surgery on her heart. So as her body slimmed down, she was stuck with the same sense of being unworthy, unlovable, and ugly, only now she didn't have her obese body to blame. Her solution? Seduction. She went to a place physically over and over with men that was catastrophic to her heart. In fact, her need for approval drove her to extremes, even to the arms of a married man, the husband of her life-long friend. When he tragically died a month later, you can imagine Linda's devastation in the middle of the deception and loss. How was she to comfort his wife when she was the "other woman"?

The *False Woman* is an idol, and a cruel one at that. As all gods require worship and the payment of alms, the *False Woman* idol demands you pay with your body, one way or the other. This idol also lives on the incense of pride and groveling.

The Trophy Woman is pretty proud of her harvest of appreciative looks, comments and nods. She looks on her less-hot sisters with feigned sadness or near disdain. Poor things, she muses. Sadly, the Invisible Woman grovels in response — yes, yes I am a poor despicable thing, she agrees.

You hear it everywhere all the time. I can't, I don't, I haven't, I couldn't. It is the sound of the heart crying I am worthless, useless, full of self pity. But honestly, this kind of groveling is nothing more than a variation of pride. Still the focus is ever on — *me*. Whether calling attention to myself or throwing off all attention, there is a heightened sensitivity to Self. The focus in on the created rather than the Creator.

Pride in either one of these forms creates walls that eventually become a prison.

And what is scary is that God opposes the proud. (James 4:7) That means He *fights* against the proud. Do you really want God fighting against you? I didn't think so. But don't think He blesses groveling either. He does not. Remember "where spirit of the Lord is, there is freedom." Maybe that is why its says that God gives grace to the humble. The hope that He holds out is a hope based on the truth of Him. There is always hope in Jesus.

But I want to make a clear distinction between groveling and humility...

Jesus was humble but He did not grovel. Not when He walked the earth. Not now.

Confidence in Humility

In Philippians 2:3-4 it says, in humility consider others better than yourself. So the Invisible Woman bows down and says "Oh I do, I do consider every woman better than me." But that is not the idea. Just as Jesus humbled himself, even to death on a cross, He did not grovel and accuse His Father of making Him junk, worthless, despicable.

He knew *exactly* who He was. He was fully God and fully man, He walked in the fullness of relationship to and with His Father. He did whatever the Father asked of Him. Not out of misery, or self-pity, or self-loathing, but in power, wisdom and grace. True humility comes from a reality of self so deep that no grade is necessary. Jesus poured out because He was free to just walk in who He was, instead of constantly measuring and gauging His success.

The *False Woman* idol, however, is wrapped up in the constant, never ending, perpetuating, without pause, 24/7, on-going, get the idea, focus on **self**. When we live on either side of the spectrum, seeking the spotlight or hiding in the shadows, we live far away from why the Lord created women and what He had in mind for them.

When you choose to live on the "How am I doing?" spectrum you live somewhere between the Trophy Woman and the Invisible Woman. But you are still living out of a lie. The whole spectrum is a lie, from one end to the other.

So it doesn't matter at what point you fall, it's still a point on a spectrum based on a lie.

God has a better way. It's called freedom. It's not that you are not aware of yourself. But you are aware of the Truth about you. For me, I began to focus on my position rather than my condition. *The Green Letters* by Miles Stanford laid out a beautiful foundation of living in who we are, our identity in Christ and what He says about us. He instructs us that this is far better than the sickening and often spiritually fatal examination of our circumstances. Our condition may be pathetic, but our position is immovable.

Position rather than condition. There is a way to live and move with Jesus so that you are more concerned and focused on His opinion than anyone else's.

And do you know what His opinion of you is?

I didn't think so.

That is why we are always on the hunt. We don't know, or believe, what the God of the universe has to say about us. We don't know who we are, because we don't know whose we are.

There is a childhood story about an ugly duckling. The plight of this duckling is that it did not look like the other ducks and so she was shamed and discarded and abused by the other ducklings in her flock. She tried very hard to be like the other ducks. But alas, she suffered terrible heartache because she was so ugly, or *unlike*, the others.

I think God would have us look more closely at the story as we look at His love. The problem of the story is not that the duckling was ugly.

The problem is that the duckling wasn't a duckling at all.

It was something altogether MORE. So are you.

The duckling failed to know, or believe the truth, because her only point of reference was the other ducks.

She kept trying live up to *their* definitions.

But she simply could not cut it as a duck.

There was a cure.

When the duckling saw what she really was, the truth of her definition, she no longer *tried* to *be* a *duck*. She could care less about the ducks. The glorious swan got a glimpse of what she really was, and what she was really becoming.

To be born in a duck's nest, in a farmyard, is of no consequence to a bird, if it is hatched from a swan's egg.

We don't need to worry about being "ugly" ducklings. We are not ducklings at all.

Christ in you the hope of glory. (Colossians 1:27)

It doesn't say the hope of being like everyone else. It doesn't even say being puffed up about your glory. It declares, proclaims, announces:

Christ.

In you.

The Hope.

Of Glory.

The Lord started telling me I wasn't a duck. And over time I believed Him.

What is God telling you? Are you tired of trying to be a duck yet?

43 — her desire

So what is the opposite of her desire will be for her husband?

Her desire will be for and BE MET in her God. Do you see how much more this resembles the garden? Her longing is so deep only her Lover, the Lord can fill it. When she is fully defined and satisfied in Him, when she embraces all *she is in Him*, then and only then is she free to release her womanhood, her True God Expression of a Woman in a relationship with a man. Her glory is restored. Or should I say, God's Glory in her is released.

Desire. This is how Jesus feels about me and about you. This intense longing. Talk about glory.

When you understand that Jesus loves us this intently, this relentlessly, then you begin to see why marriage is so important. There is nothing more powerful than when two people released in the Spirit of God come together in marriage. Talk about fireworks!

This is how it was at Meagan and Possum's wedding (their real names, I mean who would make up a name like *Possum?*).

"Glorious
over us
You shall reign
glorious"

The music rang out over the speakers. A hush settled
over the congregation.
"Glorious,
over us
You shall reign
Glorious"

And here came Meagan. She was like a bridled show
horse walking, nearly prancing, down the aisle. You
could feel the zeal and anticipation in her every step, in
her smile. Possum, her bridegroom, stood there restless,
shifting from foot to foot. Until he laid eyes on Meagan.
Then he stood stock still. Shell-shocked at the sight of her.
The only thing that moved on his body were the tears
rolling down his cheeks.

She came and stood at the foot of the altar waiting to
be given away, given to, handed to, hand in hand, to her
husband. Possum stood there, wide-eyed, mouth slightly
ajar, *drinking* her in. And Meagan glowed; she was basking,
reveling in his adoration.

It *was* glorious.

God was reigning over them in glory.

And we all felt it. It was magnetic.

Finally the moment came. The declaration. The
pronouncement. The blessing.

Husband and wife. "You may now kiss — "

But Meagan and Possum had waited so long for this kiss,
they waited no more.

Intense. Sensual but not at all shameful. The kiss was
pure — and powerful.

Everyone cheered and clapped. But the applause was for
more than the kiss.

We had all been swept up in their desire, their aching,
their intense longing to be wed, to be joined, to be one.
It was like time stopped for a few moments. And as we
rejoiced for them, a deep echo in our souls resounded: one
day, one day...a wedding awaits for us.

All was well in the world.

Why? Because when a man and a woman know who

they are in Jesus, faults and all, they come together in
God's strength, for His glory, out of His overflow — it
is truly breath-taking. It has little to do with the couple,
it has everything to do with the picture. A lovestruck
bridegroom, an eager and willing bride.

And to think His desire is for me…this kind of desire is
for me, for you…

Glorious.

Single Focus

But what if you are not married?

Then all the more — to discover who we are as women,
rather than thinking we will only be complete with a man.
I know so many women who live in this kind of "lacking"
state because they either 1) don't have a man, or 2) they
don't have a man who meets their needs.

You have a man.

A Royal Husband.

His name is King Jesus.

Have you met Him?

If you are looking for a man, try turning to the one who
is looking *for you*. As my college friends say, He is the
bomb.

His love truly satisfies.

Sisters, whether married or not, it was never the human
man's job to meet all our needs. Nor our job to meet all of
his needs. It is, however, Jesus's *desire* to meet our longings.
He longs to release and restore us, to enliven us. Then out
of this overflow we pour into others whether that is in our
relationships, marriages, families, or communities.

Ephesians 1:23 says that Jesus fills everything in *every*
way.

So what do we do with that? Sigh and say "oh well." Or
do we scratch our heads and think it must be something
we're doing wrong? Do we think "Ah ha! I need to change
men"? Or "Ah ha! I need to change *my* man"?

Or do we stop and listen?

Really listen, and hear that cry from somewhere deep within, the hunger that aches in our bellies and instead of going to the mall or the spa or the gym, go to the only source that can answer the call and satisfy the hunger.

I want to tell you three short stories about women. Like Snow White, they were all by wells. They were all approached by a man. And all were asked to do something.

Pushed Away

Moses fled from Pharaoh and went to live in Midian, where he sat down by a well.
Now a priest of Midian had seven daughters, and they came to draw water and fill the troughs to water their father's flock.
Some shepherds came along and drove them away, but Moses got up and came to their rescue and watered their flock.
When the girls returned to Reuel their father, he asked them, "Why have you returned so early today?" They answered, "An Egyptian rescued us from the shepherds. He even drew water for us and watered the flock."
"And where is he?" he asked his daughters. "Why did you leave him? Invite him to have something to eat." (From Exodus 2)

When you read this story it is easy to miss small details. These women are about their fathers's business but are pushed aside. Other shepherds come and drive them away from their work because they are women. But the Bible says that Moses got up and came to their rescue and he watered their flock.

Not only did he save them, he served them.

When Papa hears about this story what does he say? *Why did you leave him?* He sends them back. Go back to where you have been rejected and pushed aside. Go back and see this man who saves you and serves you.

Called Away

Abraham had instructed his chief servant, Eliezer, to go to his home country and find a wife for his son Isaac.

> *The girl was very beautiful, a virgin; no man had ever lain with her. She went down to the spring, filled her jar and came up again…*
>
> *"When I came to the spring today, I said, 'O Lord, God of my master Abraham, if you will, please grant success to the journey on which I have come. See, I am standing beside this spring; if a maiden comes out to draw water and I say to her, "Please let me drink a little water from your jar," and if she says to me, "Drink, and I'll draw water for your camels too," let her be the one the Lord has chosen for my master's son.'*
> *"Before I finished praying in my heart, Rebekah came out, with her jar on her shoulder.*
> *Laban and Bethuel answered, "This is from the Lord; we can say nothing to you one way or the other. Here is Rebekah; take her and go, and let her become the wife of your master's son, as the Lord has directed."*
> *When they got up the next morning, he said, "Send me on my way to my master…"*
> *But her brother and her mother replied, "Let the girl remain with us ten days or so; then you may go." Then they said, "Let's call the girl and ask her about it." So they called Rebekah and asked her, "Will you go with this man?"*
> *"I will go," she said. (From Genesis 24)*

In this story, Rebekah is just living her life. She is prepared to do the work asked of her and she is contented. So when the invitation comes from the stranger it is no small thing. It will cost her all she knows. She is being offered wealth, marriage, new land, new people, but only if she is *willing*. She has to decide which is greater: my plan or God's plan.

Swept Away

Jacob's well was there, and Jesus, tired from the journey, sat down by the well. It was about the sixth hour. When a Samaritan woman came to draw water, Jesus said to her, "Will you give me a drink?" (His disciples had gone into the town to buy food.)
The Samaritan woman said to him, "You are a Jew and I am a Samaritan woman. How can you ask me for a drink?" (For Jews do not associate with Samaritans.)
Jesus answered her, "If you knew the gift of God and who it is that asks you for a drink, you would have asked him and he would have given you living water."
"Sir," the woman said, "you have nothing to draw with and the well is deep. Where can you get this living water?"
Jesus answered, "Everyone who drinks this water will be thirsty again, but whoever drinks the water I give him will never thirst. Indeed, the water I give him will become in him a spring of water welling up to eternal life."
The woman said to him, "Sir, give me this water so that I won't get thirsty and have to keep coming here to draw water." (From John 4)

I so relate to this woman at the well. She is rejected, alone, ashamed, guilty. And here comes a Jew of all people asking her for a drink. But she still has plenty of mouth left, and asks Him why He associates with her?

Ever wonder why God associates with us?

But then comes the offer. If you knew, Jesus said. "If you knew the gift of God and who it is that asks you." She wasn't worthy. But Jesus still offered her living water.

All of these women had their lives radically interrupted. They had encounters with someone who was a foreigner, a stranger, totally unheard of. And all of these women were asked to "give" something. Go back and get him. Give him something to eat. Give me water. Give me a drink.

Their future hinged on their actions. There may have been a promise of the future, but it did not begin without a very great risk right now. Each of them stood at a crossroad. Were they willing to go the distance?

Jethro's daughters had to go back. Rebekah had to go with Abraham's servant. The Samaritan had to walk away from her sin. Don't miss this. Each woman had to move past what held her to the present, what she had formerly, until that moment, known to be real. There was a promise of something greater, but not until she had laid down her current life, what she had always known, whether good or bad. She had to decide whom she trusted.

Jesus said, *if you knew.*

Do we know who is asking us?

You probably know that the three men are pictures of God. Moses represents our defender and provider. He gives back that which is wrongly taken from us. Isaac is a picture of the promised bridegroom looking for a willing wife to come to a new land. Jesus is our Redeemer and bondage breaker. He was not stopped by her sin. He stopped her sin.

He offered her something better. Himself.

In all three stories of the women, new relationships were birthed. Moses met and married Zipporah. Rebekah indeed met and married Isaac. But don't get distracted by the man and marriage. Remember these are pictures of God. So in the final story of Jesus and the Samaritan woman, He offered her the definition of true relationship where we worship in spirit and truth.

Do you see there is no box here?

These encounters radically changed each woman's world, every future action and ultimately their future.

Ask yourself a few important questions.

Which woman at the well am I right now?

Do I need a defender? A lover? A redeemer?

What action is being asked of me?

What is the risk of this decision?

What is the cost if I say yes?

Am I willing to have my life radically changed?

You can't get to glory without a little risk. God wants to take us deeper, but it will cost us something. It will require us to go back to hard places, outside our comfort zones, and away from our sin. But "if you knew" who was asking, the process is so much easier.

My life was far from roses when I entered my own conversation about what to do with this God who asked me to give Him something. I had to decide which woman at the well am I? Would I trust Him enough to risk my fears and my dreams, my all?

44 — hard places

This season with the Lord began when we lived out in the country. I was in a crippled marriage. (Remember it's not about whether you have a man or not.) I was feeling shut down in my creative work; several of my "God projects" were now collecting dust in my basement. After years of being a Christian, I was still easily angered. I still felt as if I lived most of my relationships from a distance. My thought process was: if you really knew me, you wouldn't want to be my friend. There was still a wall I loved to hide behind.

Wait, I didn't love it anymore. Now it was so big I couldn't get around it or over it or through it. What started as a hide and seek place had become my prison.

Our family had been through a very hard year financially due to a failed business attempt and we were nearing foreclosure. Our baby who had brought such joy to our life was seriously ill. Doctor after doctor gave us no solutions. Instead we got more prescriptions that we couldn't afford and little relief. Her condition continued to worsen.

I don't want you to feel sorry for me.

I just want to make it clear that freedom has nothing to do with the prisoner — the circumstances, failures, plans, even hopes. It was not about my condition.

Freedom has to do with the one who holds the keys to the cell. Where the Spirit of the Lord is, there is freedom…

One of my steps to freedom was confronting my walls and my rationalizations. When the Lord showed me this Scripture, I could hardly ignore or justify them anymore:

> *Therefore this is what the Sovereign LORD says:*
> *In my wrath I will unleash a violent wind, and*
> *in my anger hailstones and torrents of rain will*
> *fall with destructive fury. I will tear down the*
> *wall you have covered with whitewash and will*
> *level it to the ground so that its foundation will*
> *be laid bare. When it falls, you will be destroyed*
> *in it; and you will know that I am the LORD.*
> *So I will spend my wrath against the wall and*
> *against those who covered it with whitewash.*
> *I will say to you, "The wall is gone and so are*
> *those who whitewashed it…"*
> *(Ezekiel 13:13-15)*

I know this speaks of God's wrath. But the Lord used these verses to show me just how much He *hated* my walls. How much He hated my *excuses* about my walls. I was the one who had white-washed them. He knew they were my prison and He wanted me to be free, even more than I did. But how could I ask Him to "level it to the ground" when He had also said, "you will be destroyed in it"?

Do you remember beauty from ashes?

He destroyed the False Woman Jana. I needed to be destroyed. Burnt up. Leveled to the ground.

That season of my life taught me complete and utter helplessness. I could not make my daughter heal. I could not make my husband's work turn around. I couldn't fix my marriage. I couldn't even change my own heart about how I loved people and let them love me. I couldn't do anything about my walls.

But God could. He was more than able and He was *willing*.

So what about all the mess I told you about?

That was exactly what He asked me for.

Would I give Him my fears, my dreams, my hurt? Or would I stay self protecting behind my wall, ignoring, whining, excusing? Would I go forward with Him?

I wrote out everything wrong, bad and hurting in my life. Then I rewrote it with these words preceding every line: *Lord I trust you with…*

Then I waited. For Him to speak and for things to move beyond my control.

Slowly, I stepped out from behind my wall with fear and trembling. Then with a crash He destroyed the wall, so I could never go back…

The funny thing is it took me a while to realize what had happened.

I found an old journal entry that listed what I called "hopeless situations:" the relationship with my mother-in-law, our finances, my oldest daughter's anger issues, my time management, dreams for a horse and a sailboat, ministry potential, and my weight.

"These are the same things I said last year," it said in my journal.

But instead of wallowing in self-pity, like I had the previous year, this time I had written out a series of declarations or prayers to God after each one of the problems.

Lord, do I believe You are able?

What do I dream?

What is the wildest dream in each of these circumstances?

Please do more than that.

I dream about what You made me to be.

Please, do more than that.

Don't ever let me limit You by my expectations.

I wrote out the best resolution I could think of, and then asked Him to do *more.* Just looking back over these notes encouraged me. To see how God had moved. But also to remind me that he is still moving today.

Maybe these will encourage you as well.

Doug Bannister is the pastor who stirred the idea of *expecting* from God. It changed my way of thinking about bad times or hard times or even good times. God was using every single element in my life, and still does, to make me look like Jesus. So over time, I learned not to whine or quit but to *go back to Him* and ask: how are you going to show me more of *you* in this circumstance?

Not more of the all-powerful God, which is quite impressive, but more of the up-close-and-personal God who is right in the middle of my mess with me.

Months later, when I came back to that passage about the wall from Ezekiel, my spirit buzzed on the verse, *the wall is gone and so are those who whitewashed it.*

I had to laugh in amazement. It *was* gone. Just like the burnt-up root experience, there was a tangible difference. But there's more.

Two years later as I write this, the Lord has still more to say about those walls, more to say about why He wanted the walls destroyed.

"Jerusalem *will be a city without walls…And I myself will be a wall of fire around it, declares the Lord, and I will be its glory within.*" (Zechariah 2:3)

Freedom and glory.

45 — start your bulldozer

Are you looking for three easy steps to freedom? Sorry.
I can't do that. But I *can* share with you a few tools, a few
chisels, God has used in setting me free.

• Worship

If freedom comes where His Spirit is, then ask for
His Spirit to come. One way to ask His Spirit to come is
through worship — whether that time is spent in silence,
driving down the road, or singing. One of my favorite
ways to worship is to read Scripture and then say it back or
sing it back to the Lord. Worship is an attitude of the heart.

• The Word

The Bible is living and active, sharper than any two-
edged sword. (Hebrews 4:12.) When I feel weak, sad, mad,
just yuck, I know that I am starving to death for His truth.
I feed on the Word of God. I have learned to expect God to
listen to me and to *answer* me. He has far more to say than
we have ever dared to believe. He uses the Scripture in
mighty ways. But we must come expecting. Hebrews 10:19-
23 challenges us to approach God with confidence and
with full assurance because He is faithful to hear us. You
cannot live a God-life without God's word.

• Journaling

As we write our story we see His story unfolding. As we
write out our words, He reveals His Word in the middle

of it. Journaling is a history of all God is doing in our lives. You should see the progress that has been made in my list of "hopeless situations." In every one of them you can see God's hand moving. I am so thankful that I wrote them out and then rewrote them with a blessing. In every situation, God is ever working. For His glory and my good.

Don't be lazy. And don't quit.

Ask the Lord to show you how to worship him in a deeper way. Ask the Lord to make you hungry for the Word. Ask him to reveal himself to you in a way that you can understand. You should see how many journal entries I have where God has spoken to me through nature. He took something simple that I love and used it to explain things about Himself, or me, or my circumstances.

He is very creative.

So who is this God who asks us not for something but everything?

He is the God who calls things that are not, as though they were. (Romans 4:17)

He is the Lord sings over us. (Zephaniah 3:17)

He is the Lord your God who is gracious and compassionate slow to anger and abounding in love (Exodus 34:6-7)

He is the Spirit who brings beauty from ashes. (Isaiah 61:3)

He is One who holds all things together and by whom all things are made. (Colossians 1: 15-17)

He is the God who will repay all the years that the locusts have eaten. (Joel 2:25)

He is the God who gives you His joy so that your joy may be complete. (John 15:11)

He is the God who boasts that "I will satisfy you fully." (Joel 2:19)

What do you do when the God of the universe says He will satisfy you fully?

You have a couple of options. You can walk away. Or stand there in shock. Or you can *drink Him in*. You can bank on it. Not out of disrespect.

Out of complete trust that if He said it, He means it.

Some friends of mine and I have adopted a saying, "I've been peithoed," meaning, I have been persuaded, overcome with evidence, blown away by the truth. Are you willing to be peithoed?

What exactly does peitho mean? The New Thayers Greek-English Lexicon says concerning this word peitho:

> *persuasion; to induce one by words to believe; to cause belief in a thing (which one sets forth), win one's favor; to persuade unto; i.e. move or induce someone by persuasion to do something; to suffer one's self to be persuaded; to be induced to believe; to trust."*

God peithoes us every day. He wants to get our attention. He wants us to know Him.

Why? Because all along God has been after relationship, relationship, relationship.

Another powerful way that God has peithoed me is through worship. God used worship to radically turn my world around. I spoke of this earlier. But let me take you to the next level.

46 — the more of worship

My worship journey peaked at an unusual place
called Splash Country. It is a Dolly Parton entertainment
park where the entire place, huge place, is water-related
activities. Thus the name, Splash Country. I went there
with my then-seven-year-old daughter Salem. Honestly
despite her excitement, I was dreading it. The thought of
being in a wet bathing suit and shorts for hours was not
my idea of fun. I knew that it would be a battle for my
thoughts with that much flesh flashing around. But as is
His way, the Lord had surprises up His sleeve.

Two crazy things happened for me.

First came the attack of "how is Jana doing" in the face
of so much skin and muscle. But before that lie could choke
out life, my focus was oddly — supernaturally? — shifted.
As I looked around, I got kind of lost in watching the
bodies but this time observing instead of comparing. I
saw the white and the lumpy, the bronzed and shaped, the
flabby and sculptured.

There was a wide array of the "I so got it" with lots
of bare skin proving the point, as well as lots of the "I
will never have it" covered in baggy T-shirts that clung
mercilessly when wet. But the strangest thing was they
were all standing side by side anxiously. They could hardly
walk, hardly stand still. Here was the gray-haired, the

dyed, the scarred and the nipped and tucked, all ready to go. But the anxiety was not beauty based, it was fun-based.

Normally at a place like this, there are the watchers and the doers. But today, everyone came to play, regardless of size or shape, pasty white or bottle bronzed, cool bathing suit or out-dated reruns, we all played in the water, played in the fountains, down the slides, floated down the lazy river, and huddled under the Giant bucket, which was my personal favorite.

I realized that I had joined them in the child-like excitement. But more importantly I realized I was *good* with *me*. I came to play with my daughter. And life was very good. Instead of shutting down I was able to let go and relax.

Thanks, Lord.

But then we came to the wave pool.

I just about lost all the one-with-humanity warm fuzzies when I had to stand way too close to all these near-naked bodies. I had never been to a wave pool before, so I was trying to gauge what was happening. I put down my towel on the concrete "beach" and walked into the pool of water and tried to find a place to stand with my daughter.

Now, I know that we are all made in the image of God. I am so good with that. But standing around, waiting for "something," with a bunch of wet, half-naked young and old people standing too, too close was not so good.

I mean really…

There were a lot of soggy, hairy men.

Really hairy.

Really awkward.

It was cramped and everyone was trying not to touch anyone…whew. Get the picture?

Then from over the speaker you hear this beep — beep — beep. Everyone chattered in an odd sense of anticipation and the waves begin. The water slowly rippled but then grew in momentum. It moved up and down creating waves. Up and down. Up and down. Up and down, very predictable. Up and down, very heartless. Up and down, even the kids grew bored. Up and down. Then the water went flat.

No waves. No laughter. No expectation. What do you have left? Everyone standing around cramped, wet and half-naked, trying not to touch each other — waiting.

So I take all this in and think maybe, just maybe it was a bad run at the wave pool. We hang around to see if next time is better, as if next time it would be different.

It wasn't. Not that time or the next four times.

Only the bodies changed out.

They weren't changed, they just changed out, meandered off in hopes of a little excitement.

As I stood on the wave pool edge (you could hardly call the sloped concrete a "shore"), I watched the waves go up and down in a powerless, passionless rhythm and everyone jumping on cue with feigned excitement.

Then the Lord said, *This is like worship.*

I kept watching. "How so?" I asked.

It is empty.

"Why doesn't this work, Lord? It seems like a good idea. The fun of the ocean without salt, without the sand."

Because there is no awe.

I brewed and pondered on His thought the rest of the day. And for days afterward. I taught a middle- and high-school class and we laughed about the wave pool adventure, about the concrete "shore" and the sound of everyone jumping in unison. We all jumped together in the class.

As I taught I realized one of the biggest pieces missing for me was having no ocean to look out on. There was this big fake rock mountain. I told them how silly I felt as we looked at that and yelled on cue and jumped on cue and then stood around wet, awkward, and waiting. "It was all so fake," I said to the students, "like a lot of worship."

Let's break this down. Just like a wave pool where you can jump in waves with no ocean, you can worship without a GOD to worship. When worship is not fueled by the Spirit of God, driven by desire for God, in awe of God, then it is boring and predictable and empty like the wave pool. It may be fun for a few minutes, then you wander off, ready to do something else. You are not changed by it. You just change activities.

Let's talk about the ocean. It is always different. You can't help but feel the hugeness, it is ever changing, and oh the power. I could go on and on! The smell, the feel, the taste. It never gets old, you never know what you will get when you go. Every time is different. Much like the presence of the Lord, you experience it, all of it, the feel, the taste, the smell. There is a power and source that comes in waves. But you can't control these waves. You don't even know when or how they will come. Only that they will come.

I encouraged the students to go to real worship, in awe of God, and not be satisfied with a fake wave pool kind of worship. But even after I left them, the Lord kept bringing the ocean thing back and back.

A week later I went to the beach. Is God cool or what?

Deep Calls to Deep

I stood at the ocean and I felt what I do every time, at every ocean — Awe.

With my toes curled in the sand on the shore I felt as I always do at first. Small. I looked at the sand. So white.

The Lord reminded me of the verse — more than the grains of sand, so my thoughts are of you.

No way Lord.

We continued the ocean lesson.

Look closely. What do you see?

There is life in the ocean, life I cannot see. There is power, deep power. The ocean is different every time I walk up to it. Every morning, it is different. The ocean is more than I can imagine. It goes on beyond what I can see. It refreshes me. It inspires me.

It causes me to dream again. It calls to me....

"You are Lord. You are." I whispered, simply amazed by Him.

I went back out at dusk and a storm was brewing out on the horizon. You couldn't see the clouds but you could see it on the water. It was rough, wild and restless. I stepped in the warm evening water and immediately could feel the pull; the current was strong and relentless.

> *This is how I am Jana. I come to you. Over and over. I call to you to come in. Put one little toe in and I pull you in. I take you deeper. Then bring you back to shore. But not without changing you, tumbling you around, making you a little scared and then popping you back up to the surface just in time. Even when you play at the shore, it just makes you hungry for more.*

I looked out at the expanse of the ocean. The dawning awareness that this magnificent creation is but a thimble-full compared to my God.

"What is it like out there Lord? What is it like farther out there?"

My eye strained to see every crest, looking for a dolphin. But as I peered out looking for one thing, a stingray flew happily out of the water, arching in time for a moment before it plunged back into its own world.

"Lord I strain to see one thing, and you freely give another," I whispered.

There is life out there. Abundant life.

"And here I am standing on the shore."

With a deep breath of ocean air, I walked back to my motel, my feet sinking in the cool white sand. There was a great longing in my heart.

And yet, I was somehow satisfied. For now.

The next day I was reading my Bible. The wind caught the pages and it flipped to Song of Solomon.

Lover
How beautiful you are, my darling!
Oh, how beautiful!
Your eyes behind your veil are doves.
Your hair is like a flock of goats
descending from Mount Gilead.
(Song of Songs 4:1)

I looked at it and moved on. I had studied this passage in depth. In fact I teach it. It is such a good word. I went to flip back the page.
That's for you.
I read it again. "How beautiful you my darling. How beautiful."
Yes. This is for you…Jana. You.

"Lord, don't let me get so used to telling others what you say that I don't believe it is for me anymore."

Later that day the whole family got in the car and we went to eat on the mainland. On the interstate we passed this brick wall that had two foot high letters painted on it.

YOU ARE BEAUTIFUL.

I won't let you forget.

Chuck looked over at me and smiled. "That's for you honey," he said.
"I know," I said. "I *know.*"

Because of the savour of thy good ointments
thy name is as ointment poured forth, therefore
do the virgins love thee. (Song of Solomon 1:3)

47 – the alabaster box

"What, then, is the secret?" Watchman Nee asks about worship as seen by the woman who anointed Jesus with oil.

> *Clearly it is this, that in approving Mary's ac-*
> *tion at Bethany, the Lord Jesus was laying down*
> *one thing as a basis of all service: that you pour*
> *out all you have, your very self, unto Him; and*
> *if that should be all He allows you to do, that is*
> *enough. It is not first of all a question of whether*
> *'the poor' have been helped or not. The first ques-*
> *tion is: Has the Lord been satisfied?*
> Watchman Nee,
> *The Normal Christian Life,* p. 274

You may be familiar with the story from Luke about the sinful woman who came and anointed Jesus not only with perfume but with her tears. I want you to imagine the scene.

Here is an empty chair.

The rest of the room is filled with people. Sitting in a circle, gathered in two and threes. It is humming

275

with multiple conversations. Jesus enters the scene. He is escorted by the homeowner to the empty seat. The conversational buzz is suspended for a moment as Jesus takes a seat and then all greet him. Conversations resume. Imagine the homeowner puffed and grinning at his renowned guest. Jesus is in his house no less.

But then another guest steals in quietly. Without invitation and without notice of anyone save Jesus.

Jesus is immediately aware of her. She is at His feet weeping silently. Her hot tears touch His feet like tender words of thanks and praise. She wipes them with her hair.

The homeowner, seeing that he has lost the attention of Jesus, looks for the distraction. Seeing the harlot, he starts toward the woman to grab her up and pull her away...what is such filth doing in my home, he mentally protests. But Jesus waves him off before the homeowner gets to her.

Then the woman rises, eyes still down, she goes behind Jesus and pauses. The homeowner's shoulders relax in relief. Is she leaving? he hopes, thinking that the little interruption is over. But then he draws in a breath. What was she doing now?

Tears still slide silently down her face. She raises her hands over Jesus' head. In her shaking grasp is a small white jar. An alabaster flask. Before the homeowner could refuse, she uncorks the top and a pours a soft slow trickle of oil over Jesus' head. It pools in His dark hair and then overflows down His neck. Over His brow, down His cheeks. Over His closed eyes. The oil slides down His neck, and soaks dark in His cloak. He lets out a soft slow sigh.

It is the aroma that silenced the room.

They stood speechless as the woman poured the entire flask on Jesus' head. She held it upside down, so that every drop was emptied.

The whispers began. Most missed the smile of contentment that played on Jesus' lips.

Immediately they tittered over the woman that had again taken her place at Jesus feet. They talked of her reputation. They all knew who she was and what she had done. They talked of the ridiculous cost. How on earth did she of all people get such fine perfume? They talked of her audacity. They talked of her inappropriate showiness. How dare her after all? Didn't she know who He was?

Yes she did. Precisely.

Do you?

As you walk through this scene in your mind's eye, where are you in the room? Are you the homeowner, just glad Jesus is in the house, but not really welcoming or enjoying Him? It's all for show.

Are you one of the invited guests, there to see and be seen? Are you one that is evaluating, critiquing, scoffing at the open display from the sinful woman? Does her affection make you feel jealous? Do you feel like you are on the outside looking in? Perhaps indignant? Or are you confused at what it is going on here? Does this seem outrageous, uncalled for, even…wasteful?

Are you the woman? So utterly aware of who you are and so desperately wanting to be someone else? So utterly bankrupt — physically, emotionally, spiritually — that to be seen publicly weeping is of little matter compared to the hope of His healing?

Is your need so great that you would risk everything just to show Him, somehow, that you believe He is who He says He is?

Is your love so great that you will give all you have — dreams, hopes, money, talents, reputation, beauty, everything — in a frail container to be poured out on Him for His pleasure, His enjoyment?

What does Jesus have to say about all this?

That she will be remembered.

That she has done a beautiful thing.

That her act of love (those who have been forgiven much, love much) her act of love *blessed* Jesus.

We sometimes rush through this moment to the picture of the crucifixion. Where the oil is a pre-burial rite, a foreshadowing.

But Jesus was far more present than that. He absorbs the moment of faith and affection like His garments absorbed the oil.

Then He speaks. He is a man of few words, really. So here, to declare that it is beautiful and would *always* be remembered, well, those are serious words of appreciation and affirmation.

> *He noticed her heart. Her sacrifice, her abandon.*
> *But more than merely noticing, Jesus appreciated it,*
> *enjoyed it, loved it, was impacted by it.*
> *Her loving action affected God.*
> *Jesus was satisfied.*

This is worship. This is worship in spirit and truth. In the Greek, worship means *pros kuneos*. A kiss toward. Do we kiss Jesus in worship? Is He satisfied because He knows we have held nothing back?

Hoarding Boxes

I was taking inventory of my own alabaster boxes. There were boxes that held my dreams, gifts, love, service, time, my passions, even a box that is about caring for myself. And I noticed there are boxes I try to hide from the Lord (my dreams and passions), the ones I don't pour out *everything* but only what I think is enough (my love and service), and the ones that I put on the shelf to use "later" (my gifts and caring for myself).

I didn't really view myself as an abandoned woman...

A mighty conversation began with the Lord.

I was calling out to Him, telling Him how I want to pour out, how I want to be filled up to overflowing so that He will spill out on those around me, how I want to take care of the little flock He had given. All these emotions and prayers poured out of my heart. My ardent prayer ended with one rush of words "Lord I want to make a difference."

And His reply was deafening.

*I want to make **you different**.*

I was stopped in my tracks. I heard the two comments. One was laborious, one was freeing. When I *try* to make a difference then the effort is up to me, on my shoulders. But when it is Jesus *making me different* the journey is totally *other*, totally Him.

God making me different is a God thing. And as He makes me different, all the other desires, hopes, and goals will play out for His glory.

His glory life in me makes all the difference.

What better evangelical tool is there than a person who is radically different because of the presence of Jesus Christ? What can be a more powerful story than a life that has been changed? Look at the woman at Jesus's feet.

Was the woman changed?

Jesus said, Your sins are forgiven, go in peace.

This isn't just peace like, have a Coke and a smile. This is complete restoration, total healing, the broken made whole.

> But whenever anyone turns to the Lord, the veil is
> taken away. Now the Lord is the Spirit, and where
> the Spirit of the Lord is, there is freedom. And
> we, who with unveiled faces all reflect the Lord's
> glory, are being transformed into his likeness with

ever-increasing glory, which comes from the Lord,
who is the Spirit. (2 Corinthians 3:16-18)
I love this. We turn to Him. He transforms us. Glory to glory.

Love lifted *me*.
Love *lifted* me.
When nothing else would help.
Love lifted me.

48 — ash work

Part of the power of this story is the woman's
willingness to claim her sin and then her willingness to lay
it at His feet. Before there can be beauty for ashes, there has
to be the ash work.

Wait a minute. Ashes? Girl — I've got ashes.

We say as women, "Listen, I've already got ashes, I have
burned every bridge, scorched every relationship, singed
every dream. I got ashes."

But this is a little different. You have to put a name to the
ashes.

Name the attempts: controlling, neglecting, hiding.

Name the false gods: food, sex, clothes, rejection,
religion, pride, beauty, relationships.

Name the hurts and disappointments: parents,
girlfriends, work, weight, the man, dreams.

Then set them on fire. Burn them thoroughly until
they are ashes. Burned up. Not recognizable. Burned up
ambition. Burned up pride, burned up beauty, burned up
self.

Once that is a pile of dust at your feet, then it becomes
the alabaster box. Because there is nothing left but the
pure nard, or fragrant oil. All that is left is a broken and
contrite spirit. What an aroma. It is death to those who are
perishing, those in the room with Jesus, but to those who

are alive, it is the aroma of Christ. (2 Corinthians 2:15)

True worship smells like this.

The best of what you have poured out on Him. And then, holding your breath, you wait for His reaction.

Your heart seizes up as you sense the onlookers' reactions: disgust, scorn, comparison.

But still you keep your eyes on Him, waiting, hoping, willing to keep the oil pouring down His head, on His cheeks. Then you see the oil mingling with tears...His tears, your tears.

And you both bask in the reality that this is the most important thing. You both are blessed that you have poured out all you have for Him no matter what the others say.

No matter what else it could have been used for.

You both know, He is worth all that and *more*.

One of the greatest side effects to this kind of worship is seeing how abandon changes the room.

Did it matter then? Evidently.

Does it matter now? Obviously.

He inhabits the praises of His people. There is that dwelling, living among us thing again.

This matters to Jesus so much that He says this act of worship will be remembered always. This satisfaction is not a checklist being done. Or a dutiful father patting a daughter on the head.

This is a contented sigh, a deep inward groan of a lover...*satisfied*.

Yes, Lord make me different. And that will make all the difference.

It will for you too.

Christ in me, in you, the hope of glory.

Glory to the Father of all.

49 — dwelling place

This may sound like heresy. But if you have stuck with me this far, maybe you won't be too shocked. Remember Immanuel? Do you remember what that means?

God with us. Or the God who dwells with us.

All through the Bible, it is His proclamation, His intent, His plan. Talk about a purpose driven life...

> *For the Lord has chosen Zion,*
> *he has desired it for his dwelling:*
> *"This is my resting place for ever and ever;*
> *here I will sit enthroned, for I have desired it —*
> *(Psalm 132:13)*

> *And I heard a loud voice from the throne saying,*
> *"Now the dwelling of God is with men, and he*
> *will live with them. They will be his people, and*
> *God himself will be with them and be their God.*
> *(Revelation 3)*

> *Sing and rejoice, O daughter of Zion: for, lo, I*
> *come, and I will dwell in the midst of thee, saith*
> *the LORD. (Zechariah 2:10, KJV)*

Then came the song, *Better is One Day.*

How lovely is Your dwelling place,
oh Lord Almighty
My soul longs and even faints for You
For here my heart is satisfied,
within Your presence
sing beneath the shadow of Your wings
Better is one day in Your courts
Better is one day in Your house
Better is one day in Your courts
Than thousands elsewhere (thousands elsewhere)
One thing I ask and I would seek,
to see Your beauty
To find You in the place Your glory dwells
My heart and flesh cry out,
for You the living God
Your spirit's water for my soul
I've tasted and I've seen,
come once again to me
I will draw near to You
I will draw near to You

One day during worship we were singing that song. And the Spirit of the Lord asked me, *"Jana where is my dwelling place?"*

I had to stand there for a moment. And then all kinds of Scripture flashed in my mind:

Christ in you the hope of glory (Col. 1:27)

We will come to him and make our home with him (John 14:23)

Hidden in Christ (Col 3: 1-3)

We are His body (I Corinthians 12:27)

Where is His dwelling place? Inside me?

And then the words from the song surround me again. *How lovely is your dwelling place...*Well am I lovely then?

Are you?

Before you read that as grossly egotistical, try reading that with wonderment. Try reading that first of all, that God would *want* to dwell with us. And second, that He *does* in fact dwell in us. And third of all, since He dwells in us, the character of Him must be *in* us, His beauty, His love, *His glory.*
What do *you* do with that?

How lovely is your dwelling place...

You know what I do with that? I look at God's dwelling places very, very differently.
I ask the Lord to give me His eyes. My eyes are seduced by the world. I want His eyes when I look at me, and when I look at others.

50 — a new name

I cannot know if this was an act of rejection, protection or compassion but Adam gave a new name to Woman. He called her Eve, which means living. Once they shared the same name, Adam, the same oneness, fellowship and closeness. And now in the gaping reality of the brokenness, a new name seems the most logical solution.

But new names are not always a sign of separation. In fact, there is something powerful in a name.

I know we sought the Lord about what to name our children. We wanted His take on who He was creating. So we listened carefully for His leading. We wanted to bless our children with names that mattered. Names that meant something. Names that conveyed God working in their lives even before they were born. Names that would be a banner over them, a proclamation of God over their lives.

My friends think I am way too intense. But it's biblical.

All through the Bible, God names people, and God changes people's names. Abram to Abraham, Jacob to Israel, Sari to Sarah, John the Baptist, Gomer's children, even the names given to Jesus.

Good or bad. Rachel on her deathbed named her newborn, Ben-Oni, son of my trouble. Thankfully, dad stepped in and named him Benjamin, son of my right hand. What a difference a name makes.

So the Lord loves names.

Why? Because God uses names to describe and explain himself. Names are forms of identification.

What's in a name? *Everything* when you are talking about God.

I have a calendar, a 365 day calendar, that has a different name of God for each day. Timothy Botts created this masterpiece called, "I Am." 365 names. Not a description. A name. I am sure 365 names are still not all the names of God. But 365 names helps me get my little mind around who He is.

So, when my friend John Dee prayed over us a blessing that the power of God be revealed and that there be a release of gifts, and new names, I was intrigued and a little clueless.

After the prayer I asked John, "What is that? A new name?"

And in true John Dee fashion, he told me to go to Jesus and the Word and see what I found. I started digging in Scripture and it is very frequent. In fact, commonplace.

It is everywhere. I will name you, I will call you. And there is specific Scripture about God giving us new names. Lots of Scripture. Here is one:

"You will be called by a new name that the mouth of the Lord will bestow." (Isaiah 62:2)

So I asked Him to tell me my name. I knew how important my children's names were to me. I am His child, so it stands to reason that *my* name is important to *Him*. I asked. Simple as that. Then I waited.

I heard John's wife Sue relate her name story. And then I heard testimony after testimony of how He gave or revealed names. My asking moved from casual to fervent.

And the day it came, I just sat there. This is a little too close to my heart for public consumption. But I want to tell you how amazing it is when the Living God gives you a name. In true fashion for me, I didn't believe I had heard Him right.

I asked Him to tell me again so I could be sure it was Him. The Lord was really good about it. He did. Over and over.

Guess what? The Lord does not stutter.

Now a couple of years have passed and I have watched the Lord reveal himself in amazing ways through a given name to many people. Through a Scripture, or a picture, or prayer, or a small still voice.

To not only be called out but called out specifically, intentionally, uniquely, does something to your soul. His name for us is like His plan for things to come.

People are always dumbfounded. Here are some names the Lord has given in lots of different ways to people I know personally.

Sought After, Butterfly, Faithful, Doxa, Repairer of Broken Walls, Sunshine, Pearl.

These are all real people with real encounters with a Real God.

How do you think your thoughts about *you* would change if you heard what the Lord God Almighty called you? Why don't ask Him?

See if this doesn't help you step out of your boxes.

Every one of these people scratched their head and said, Huh? Me? But the Lord used the name to drive truth deep down in their souls.

If I told you these names were given to people who struggled with infidelity, promiscuity, rejection, worthlessness, being victims of child abuse, would you be able to connect the dots?

All they could see was pain and struggle and hurt. And then God says, *"Wait just a minute. This is who I see. This is who you really are."*

Remember that hunk of marble. God sees the original intent. He knows what we are becoming. And He loves it.

It brings the promises of God to a whole new level.

"The one who calls you is faithful. He will do it."

That gets me pretty fired up. When you tell me what you

see in me, it is really cool. When the God of heaven and earth tells me what He sees in me, I am off the charts! Why don't you ask Him yourself...what's your name?

Glory

Now what does this have to do with my glory, your glory?

We are settling for crumbs when we can have a feast. God is offering us a lot more than we are taking. We are settling for churchianity instead of intimacy. We are settling for stereotypes in and out of the church instead of being defined by the Creator. We are bickering over roles when God is calling us to be warriors for the Kingdom of God.

I am my Beloved's and His desire is toward me.

I am my beloved's and he is mine.

I know who I am and whose I am and He is fully taken with me. He is the Beholder. He is the Author, the Finisher. He is the only one who matters. He is my all in all. He is the Lover that I have always longed for.

He is the Source. He is the Redeemer.

In my language He is the Curse Breaker.

He is my satisfaction so that out of this overflow, my relationship to everyone else is changed.

My marriage is different because Jesus has my heart.

My parenting is different because Jesus has my heart.

Everything flows from His source, instead of me trying to scramble around to grab some affirmation here and approval there, definition here or there.

And in an unusual God-like way, this knowledge helped me to be more of a woman. I stepped off the *False Woman* spectrum. No more bouncing between the Trophy and Invisible Woman. I am free to express my glory, my womanhood without all the fear of rejection.

I pushed down the walls of my church boxes. I can trust the Lord to lead and define and defend me.

He said, His gifts and callings are irrevocable.

I believe Him.

There is such freedom in these revelations. I don't have to be a quiet little church lady. I don't have to be a desperate False Woman trying to get some man to fill up my ever-leaking self-esteem tank. I don't have to have children by natural childbirth to prove I am a female of worth. I don't think that is what God had in mind when He made Woman. He had in mind lots of colors, lots of creative splashes, lots of His glory...

I remember telling my husband to fasten His seat belt, because I was getting ready to let my glory out. You should have seen the look on His face.

Like the Visa® ad, it was priceless.

Understanding God's glory in me has changed my whole perspective about everything, everyone.

I told a room of 20-something-year-old women that it feels like Jesus has washed my face; He has carefully but intently scrubbed off the lies and heartache and rejection caked on my face, and then rinsed it with His living water, and with my face cupped gently in His hands, He smiles and whispers, "Oh, there you are."

Do I have doubts or fears or angst at times? Sure. But I know what it feels like to have a clean face. So I go back to Him, time and again, and ask Him to wash me with the water of His Word.

When the Beast is on the prowl, I pick up my sword. And in the name of Jesus, I stand. I call out the lies and burn them up and pour them out as worship. Beauty for ashes.

Then I remember, my royal husband delights in my beauty...

a city that has God as a wall of fire and His glory within.....

I get to be fully the Jana Woman God thought of.

And that is honestly a little scandalous.

Scandalous as in extravagant. Out there.

Unleashed.

Unhindered.

Unhindered

It was glory that was promised
and glory that was lost
And it was glory restored again
through the blood shed on the cross
So let us take hold of all you've given
A hold of you've done

We would be free in you Jesus

I'm surrendered to
the Beauty of who You are
Unhindered in the image
of my Father's heart
I'm dancing in the freedom
of my Lover's arms

We are free in you Jesus
We are free in you Jesus

(Jana Spicka, Unhindered
Worship © 2007)

Additional Scriptures for Prayer and Meditation:

Isaiah 62:3

Isaiah 43:1

Isaiah 46:4

Jeremiah 9:23-24

Isaiah 54:4-5

Isaiah 41:10

Isaiah 61

Psalm 90:17 KJV

2 Corinthians Chapter 3

Appendix A

One of the greatest problems in dealing with sexual addiction is ignorance. Of men and women. If you throw the "addict" word on anything people run in the other direction, even though there really is an addiction. Therefore, I suggest you read this. Be armed so you can pray, so you can counsel, so you can take your place in this war against men, marriage and ultimately, women.

Douglass Weiss and his ministry have great and life changing resources. The following is information found on his website. Please see it for additional resources and help.

For more information see www.sexaddict.com

1. WHAT IS SEX ADDICTION?
Sex addiction is a way some people medicate their feelings and/or cope with their stresses to the degree that their sexual behavior becomes their major coping mechanism for stresses in their life. The individual often can not stop this sexual behavior for any great length of time by themselves. The sex addict spends a lot of time in the pursuit of his or her sexual behavior/fantasy or they may have a binge of sexual behaviors.

2. WHY DO PEOPLE BECOME SEXUALLY ADDICTED?
This is different for every sex addict but generally speaking there are biological, psychological, and spiritual reasons. The following is a short explanation of each reason why someone can become a sex addict. The biological addict is someone who has conditioned their body to receive endorphins and enkephlines (brain chemicals) primarily through reinforcing a fantasy state with the ejaculation that provides these chemicals to their brain. Psychologically, the need to medicate or escape physical, emotional or sexual abuse can demand a substance, the early addict finds the sex medicine usually before alcohol or drugs. Spiritually, a person is filling up the God hole in them with their sexual addiction. The addiction is their spirituality, it comforts them, celebrates them and is always available and present. Then there is the sex addict who can be two or even three of the above reasons. This is why a specialist in sex addiction is the best route for recovery with sex addiction.

3. WHAT'S THE DIFFERENCE BETWEEN SEX ADDICTION AND A HIGH SEX DRIVE?

I have heard this question on almost every national talk show or radio show I have been on over the years. A person with a high sex drive is satisfied with sex. It's not about a fix for something; when their partner says "NO" it doesn't make them go off the handle thinking their partner is totally rejecting them and have to leave the house or act out in some other way. If you can relate to this the chances are there may be an addiction issue.

4. CAN YOU BE ADDICTED TO MASTURBATION?

Yes, this is by far the most common sex addiction that I have treated in working with sex addiction. This usually is the first sexual behavior many of us will have on a repeated basis. This is usually where the sexual compulsion starts with sex addicts and this behavior, regardless of other acquired behaviors, usually stays active.

5. WHAT ROLE DOES PORNOGRAPHY PLAY IN SEX ADDICTION?

Pornography for many sex addicts combined with regular masturbation is the cornerstone for most sex addicts. Many sex addicts have great difficulty getting sober from this combination of behavior. The pornography with fantasy creates an unreal world that the sex addict visits throughout their adolescence and other developmental stages and creates an object relationship that conditions their emotional and sexual self to depend upon these objects and fantasies to meet their emotional and sexual needs hundreds of times before having sex with a real person.

6. CAN SOMEONE BE A SEX ADDICT AND NOT BE SEXUAL WITH THEIR SPOUSE OR COMMITTED RELATIONSHIP?

YES! We call this later stage of sex addiction, sexual anorexia. In this stage of sex addiction, the addict prefers the fantasy world and fantasy sex with themselves or others instead of relational sex with their spouse or partner. The addict/anorexic avoids relational sex and hence this couple has sex infrequently and often at the partners request not the addict/anorexics.

7. WHAT IS IT LIKE TO LIVE WITH A SEX ADDICT FROM A PARTNER'S OR WIFE'S PERSPECTIVE?

The partners/wives of sex addicts report many similar feelings about living with the sex addict. The feeling of aloneness is a common experience with partners of sex addicts, the sense that he can't open up and tell you about his "real" self. The confusion of even after you do certain behaviors that this still is not enough and the hopelessness that there isn't enough. Anger for many different unmet needs as a person and as a woman are often common.

8. CAN PARTNERS GET HELP EVEN IF THE SEX ADDICT DOESN'T?

Yes, even if the addict stays in denial of their addiction the partner can receive help and support for herself. The feelings of anger, loss, loneliness and many other feelings encountered over the years of living with this addiction will effect a person. These feelings need to be dealt with therapeutically whether they stay married to the addict or not. If you would like a telephone counseling appointment call (719) 278-3708 to get setup. The addiction was in no way your doing as a partner or wife, the addicts addiction started many years before you even met your addict. This addiction would have grown and damaged anyone they would have related to in any relationship. You can subscribe to our Partners Newsletter.

9. IS THERE RECOVERY FOR SEX ADDICTION?

Yes, there is recovery for sex addiction. This recovery takes time and hard work especially in the first year but with guided help the sex addict can experience restoration in their emotional, relational, sexual, financial and even spiritual lives. I have seen marriages made better than they ever were and addicts live much happier lives than they ever thought possible. I have been in successful recovery over eleven years and I know it's available for those who choose to work for and maintain recovery. If you would like a telephone counseling appointment call (719) 278-3708 to get setup.

10. IS THERE RESEARCH ON SEX ADDICTION AVAILABLE?

There is research being done in the field of sexual addiction. The monitored mail list of Heart to Heart Counseling centers provides weekly research information as well as excerpts from 101 Practical Exercises for sexual addiction recovery as well as Twelve Step discussions.

11. CAN WOMEN BE SEX ADDICTED?

Yes! The number of women desiring treatment is growing significantly. The behaviors are the same as their male counterparts including: masturbation, pornography, internet activity, anonymous encounters and affairs. Over twenty recovering female sex addicts contributed in writing She Has a Secret: Understanding Female Sexual Addiction. This book plus the Secret Solutions Workbook, with over 115 helpful techniques for recovery is just for her. If you would like to set up a telephone counseling appointment to start your journey of recovery, call today. There is hope for female sex addicts to recovery.

12. IS THERE ANY WAY TO HELP OUR CHILDREN NOT BECOME SEXUALLY ADDICTED?

Yes! Even though many of our adult male clients report that their fathers were sex addicts (porn, affairs, prostitutes etc.) they also report getting little to no proper sexual information to balance their sexual perspective. Good Enough to Wait is the first video of this kind to help your children understand sex and the brain, the long-term affects of pornography, long term sexual satisfaction and a whole lot more. This is the best combination of sex research and spiritual principles to date for youth to watch to give them a proper and currently informed sex talk.

About the Author

Jana Spicka is an author, speaker and songwriter. She spent several years abroad before returning to Knoxville, Tennessee where she makes her home with her husband, Chuck and their two daughters, Salem and Charis.

She is a graduate of Maryville College and a member of Fellowship Evangelical Free Church. Jana's passion for the next generation has been poured out on thousands of students in schools, assemblies, and conferences. She produces abstinence materials that are used across the US and Canada. In addition to *Unhindered*, she wrote *The Locket and the Mask*, a children's book promoting self-esteem and purity.

Jana recorded her first worship CD, *Daughters of Song*, in 2002, and her second CD, *Unhindered*, in 2007. Her song, *Life is Sacred*, was part of the Sanctity of Life package available through Focus on the Family. She was featured on *Family Life Today* for the booklet *Celebrating Jesus, How to Keep Christ in Christmas*.

Editing, publishing and other literary services.

(865) 254-5835
dpatrick@visionrun.com
www.visionrun.com